GREAT at LinkedIn

Tips, Tricks, and Hacks to be GREAT at the World's Largest B2B Social Platform

By Mike Sweigart

Copyright © 2020 by Mike Sweigart

All rights reserved. No part of this publication may be reproduced, distributed, or transmitted in any form or by any means, including photocopying, recording, or other electronic or mechanical methods, without the prior written permission of the publisher, except in the case of brief quotations embodied in critical reviews and certain other noncommercial uses permitted by copyright law.

The information contained in this book is for your information only. There are no guarantees regarding the level of success experienced by readers. Each person's level of success depends on their motivation, background, experience, and desire.

Although the author and publisher have made every effort to ensure that the information in this book was correct at press time, the author and publisher do not assume and hereby disclaim any liability to any party for any loss, damage, or disruption caused by errors or omissions, whether such errors or omissions result from negligence, accident, or any other cause.

TABLE OF CONTENTS

Acknowledgements 1
Introduction 5

Section 1 - Why Use LinkedIn? A Little Bit of History 13
    Section 1.1 - LinkedIn's Humble Beginnings and Growth 13
    Section 1.2 - Growing With LinkedIn 15
    Section 1.3 - LinkedIn By the Numbers 17

Section 2 - Getting Started With Your Profile 19
    Section 2.1 - Profile Visibility And Contact Info 21
    Section 2.2 - Background Photos 24
    Section 2.3 - Your Profile Picture 29
    Section 2.4 - Profile Picture Tools to Use 34
    Section 2.5 - Creating the Best First Impression With Taglines 36
    Section 2.6 - How to Turn the About Section Into a Client Magnet 44
    Section 2.7 - Professional & Volunteer Experience 49
    Section 2.8 - Education, Certificates, and Courses 52
    Section 2.9 - Skills, Endorsements, and Recommendations 53
    Section 2.10 - Interests 55
    Section 2.11 - Final Profile Tips 57

Section 3 - Turning Content Into Your Personal Gold Mine 59
    Section 3.1 - Writing Content For LinkedIn 60
    Section 3.2 - Crafting Thought Leadership Articles 62

Section 3.3 - Article Checklist 74
Section 3.4 - Using Posts 76
Section 3.5 - Excellent Third-Party Apps to Make Your Content Shine 79

Section 4 - Networking 83
    Section 4.1 - Connecting with your existing network.. 84
    Section 4.2 - How to Use Your Education / Work Experience to Expand Your Network 89
    Section 4.3 - How to Connect After someone has viewed your profile 91
    Section 4.4 - Networking with inMail messages 94
    Section 4.5 - How to Craft Highly Effective Intro Messages 96
    Section 4.6 - Commenting Your Way to the Top ... 99
    Section 4.7 - How to Engage In and Have a Presence in Groups 103
    Section 4.8 - Continuing the conversation after the connection 105

Section 5 - Additional LinkedIn Services 109
    Section 5.1 - LinkedIn Premium Business 110
    Section 5.2 - The Basics of LinkedIn Navigator ... 112

Section 6 - Conclusion 117

ACKNOWLEDGEMENTS

I wasn't sure if I was ever actually going to write a book. I really thought writing books was for people that were, you know, great writers. Literary heroes like the Jane Austens and the Charles Dickens and the John Grishams of the world.

People much smarter than me.

Things changed, though.

As I got deeper and deeper into LinkedIn and learned all about the little idiosyncrasies that could be valuable to my friends, I knew that this book was definitely going to happen.

There are a lot of people along the way that helped inspire me to get where I am in the publishing of this book.

Without a doubt, my biggest inspiration and the pillar of my life is my wife Donna. She fell in love with this knucklehead kid 27 years ago in Auburn, Alabama. Since then, we've evolved and developed as human beings together. It's absolutely amazing to have someone who unconditionally loves me.

When it comes to my family, my oldest daughter, Emma, has been doing some final editing of this book. I appreciate her so much for helping me.

There's also my son, Reed, who is one of the most kind, intelligent people in the world. He's also one of the best sounding boards I've ever met in my entire life. He has been a huge inspiration and gave me a big push for this book.

When it comes to editors, I couldn't do any of this without my dear friend and partner on this book, Emily Hunter. She is amazing and talented, really keeping me organized and focused on getting this out into the world.

This book is for business people, and I would be remiss if I didn't mention some amazing people who inspired me to push forward on this book.

Teak Shore from Southern Lighting Source has been a great friend and mentor.

John Flood from Flood Brothers has always seen something in me even when I didn't see it in myself. He's going to get one of the very first copies of this book and I'm super excited to have him be a part of it.

I could go on and on about the people who have affected me and inspired me to write this.

One of the people who really inspired me to piss or get off the pot is Akbar Sheikh. He is the leader of my mastermind, a friend, and a realist... a practicalist if that's a word. He said, 'hey man, this is what you're going to do, and this is how you do it.'

There are a couple of other dear friends I would definitely like to recognize that always inspired me to be great at sales, be creative, and push forward. My friends Don Knapp and John Schaeffer. These are two guys that are super talented, super intelligent, that always make me keep my game at its highest.

And here's the real inspiration for this book.

My real inspiration comes from how much I love to help make other people's lives better. Whether that's through humor, education, or simplifying something that's complicated like online marketing and possibly making it a little easier.

I'm hoping this book will make it a little easier for you to fill your pipeline or close that next deal. I hope you enjoy it and thank you to all the people who were a huge part of this book.

I love you all.

INTRODUCTION

LinkedIn is by far the most potent business social media platform on the planet. Think about it: you've got a gigantic captive audience who are all in "business mode," eager to learn about your products and services - and willing to pay for them. Your LinkedIn profile, when optimized, can be your primary networking and sales machine.

Best of all, it works 24/7. 365 days a year.

LinkedIn has the potential to be an amazing tool for networking and growth, but only for the people who know what to do to make it happen. That's what you'll learn from this book.

By applying the information here, your experience on LinkedIn will be far better. Just understanding the potential of the platform opens the door up for nearly **infinite branding and sales opportunities** for you. By tweaking your profile, writing more engaging posts and articles, and networking with intent, you'll be able to propel yourself to the ROCKSTAR 1 percent!

In this book, we'll show you how to use LinkedIn the right way. You'll learn how to build curiosity about who you are and about your services. You'll also learn how to address your ideal audience's problems, and how to leverage LinkedIn to help someone move down through your sales funnel, so that they trust you enough to become your client when the time comes.

All the tips, tricks, and hacks within this book are designed to get people to connect with you or your business. My goal is to turn you into a lead-generating, full-schedule-creating, networking magnet.

Can I absolutely, positively guarantee success with LinkedIn? No. Will everything that you do turn out to be a barn-busting viral success? Nope. I can say that if you're consistent with taking action, chances are high that you'll gain traction with your message and increase your business.

You HAVE to be an action taker.

How Do We Generate More Clicks, Calls, and Clients with LinkedIn?

To use LinkedIn to its fullest, keep the following principle consistently at the top of your mind. You'll see it come up over and over throughout the course of this book, and that's no accident. Following it opens up the doors, windows, living rooms, and (most importantly) pocketbooks of client love and adoration.

Are you ready for it?

Everything you do on LinkedIn has to be about YOUR AUDIENCE and your potential clients, not about YOU.

Dale Carnegie says it best in his global bestseller *How to Win Friends and Influence People*:

> "People [...] try to wigwag other people into becoming interested in them. Of course, it doesn't work. People are not interested in you. They are not interested in me. They are interested in themselves—morning, noon, and after dinner."

The ultimate goal, the secret to 'winning' at the LinkedIn game, centers around how much value you can deliver to others. With this goal in mind, you can use your LinkedIn profile to endear yourself to your prospects, whether in a B2B, B2C, or B2Me setting.

Everything that you present should look like a win-win situation for the people who should be hiring you.

Think of it like fishing. You don't put your favorite food on the hook. You don't attach a sticky note explaining to the fish how hungry you are and how great it would be to have a fried fish sandwich for dinner. You attach the bait the fish will wants. You have to think like a fish to catch a fish.

We'll be returning to this principle again and again in the book, so keep it in mind.

Before we continue, I'd like to give you a little more about my history with LinkedIn, why I wrote this book about it, and why I think that it's one of the most powerful business platforms on the planet.

From Door-to-Door to Half a Billion in Sales

I got my start in sales when I was 12. I was selling candy and glycerine soaps door-to-door, getting restocked out of the skeeziest white-paneled appliance van on the planet, and getting paid a fortune to do it - or what seemed like a fortune at the time!

For a while, I was a significant breadwinner for my family. I'd help out with paying the power bill, groceries, and more. If I wanted to get something, I was able to get it with my own money.

My father was an entrepreneur and business owner several times over, but he wasn't very good at it. Fortunately for me, you can learn a lot from seeing other people make mistakes, and I have been able to take the things that I learned from him and turn them into gold. Life gave me plenty of lemons, so I got really good at making lemonade.

In my lifetime, I've sold over half a BILLION dollars worth of goods and services, from candy to lighting and commercial furniture, and everything in between.

Sales is in my blood.

Let's jump from the early 1980s to 2003.

LinkedIn had just hit the market and was getting a bit of buzz. It was supposedly the platform to use if you wanted to get your resume out there, wanted to make business connections, or hire someone. It was *supposedly* all that and a bag of Cheetos.

Now, I've always been eager for opportunities to grow

my business. So, I set up my LinkedIn profile, put my picture on there, uploaded my resume, and launched it.

What did I get? Crickets.

I didn't even know what I was expecting to happen, but "nothing at all" wasn't it. There was no fanfare. People weren't coming to me in droves. And sure, I connected with my friends, but that wasn't going anywhere. They already knew how to contact me.

I let it go as a tool. Sure, I was still connecting with new people off and on, but I didn't take LinkedIn seriously. It wasn't doing anything, right? My profile sat there for 6 years.

Until I had an opportunity.

The world looked different, to say the least. Facebook was taking the world by storm, and people were approaching digital interactions in an entirely new way. I had just gotten a new job in commercial real estate. It was a new industry for me, and I didn't know any of the movers and shakers in my area. Forget movers and shakers - I didn't know **anyone.** I had to find some contacts fast.

Thinking back to my time in 2003, I decided to give LinkedIn another chance - this time, with a goal in mind. I wanted over 500 connections.

Why 500? Once you get past 500 connections, it doesn't matter how many you have. On your profile, it just says 500+ connections.

So, I got to work. Over the next several months, I learned about LinkedIn by pursuing this goal.

I networked like crazy for months, and my business and connections blew up. But I gained more than just connections. I saw my bottom line grow by leaps and bounds by following up on those connections. I soon found myself making real estate deals.

I started to see the power of LinkedIn, but I wanted to get a bit deeper.

When I discovered sales funnels, I wondered where LinkedIn fit into them. I became really interested in conversion rate optimization. Just WHAT types of pictures worked in the profile best? WHAT kinds of articles could I write that would move the needle? HOW could I create my LinkedIn landing page so it would bring people in?

That's what's important - bringing people in. Starting a conversation. What's the point of a beautiful landing page if it doesn't take people to the next step?

Now, I do a lot of sales training throughout the country. And each time I do training, I talk about LinkedIn and how well it's been working for me. Naturally, I've received a bunch of follow-up questions, many of which can be boiled down to this one:

"How do you use LinkedIn for branding and sales?"

I found myself answering with a lot of the same responses.

- Are there calls to action on your landing page?
- Does your profile show credibility in your field?
- Does it speak to your ideal audience?

- Does your page develop enough curiosity in your ideal audience that it could lead them away from their current provider based on what you're offering?
- Does your tagline clearly state what you do and generate curiosity?
- Are you using your picture and is it a good one?
- Are you using an appropriate cover picture?

All of these tweaks (among others), all of these golden nuggets of information that you'll learn how to leverage in this book, turn LinkedIn into an incredibly powerful lead and sales generation machine.

As you reach out and make more connections, you'll find that LinkedIn's algorithm will start to help you by pulling you up on more searches. This increased exposure allows you to make more connections. It becomes a snowball rolling downhill into an avalanche of sales.

And you don't even have to spend a lot of money to do it either. Although there are tools that you can use to make it even easier (we'll talk about those toward the end of the book), they aren't necessary to achieve success on LinkedIn. They just make it faster and easier.

So... what are you waiting for?

What You Can Expect From This Book

This book is designed to take you from being a total novice in LinkedIn and give you the tools that you need to make a positive impression on your peers and your prospects. Each section builds on the next to help you create your own sales generation system on LinkedIn.

Section 1 digs into the history of LinkedIn and its importance to the business world, clueing you in on the context of the platform.

Section 2 dives into the most basic - yet most important - part of the system: your profile. Here, you'll learn how to craft the best prospect-attracting page possible, no matter your niche.

Section 3 revolves around content creation, which is what ultimately draws people on LinkedIn to your profile. We'll go over which types of content create true results and how you can leverage your LinkedIn content creation beyond just this platform.

Section 4 talks about how to network the right way using LinkedIn. I'll show you how to use the same strategies that helped me grow my profile beyond 500 connections, while avoiding all my mistakes. You'll learn how to strengthen your connections and use LinkedIn Groups to your advantage.

Section 5 deals with additional services that LinkedIn offers to help you go even further. We'll talk about LinkedIn Premium Business and Navigator, powerful tools that you can use for branding and sales.

Thank you for reading this introduction! Let's start out by getting into a bit of history.

SECTION 1 - WHY USE LINKEDIN? A LITTLE BIT OF HISTORY

"Effective communication is 20% what you know and 80% how you feel about what you know." - Jim Rohn

Section 1.1 - LinkedIn's Humble Beginnings and Growth

It's very unlikely that you're reading this book without knowing what LinkedIn is in the first place. So why the history lesson? It's simple. LinkedIn has gone through so many changes over its lifetime that many people don't realize what an incredible platform it's become, and even those that know how it's evolved haven't been able to keep up with current best practices.

Most people in the professional world today have a LinkedIn profile. Despite this, it still seems like a Wild

West at times, and I'm constantly amazed at the variety of ways in which people behave on LinkedIn. I've talked to hundreds of professionals that are on the platform today, and I've discovered many misconceptions surrounding what the platform does and how it should be used.

Many of these misconceptions have grown from LinkedIn's history. Let's review how the platform got its start and how these misconceptions grew, so we can correct our ideas of what LinkedIn is for.

LinkedIn started back in 2003, but it was nothing like the platform we know today. In those early days, it really was just a place to post your resume, and had only a few thousand users. Most of the features of LinkedIn were designed for you to connect with people you already knew. HR teams could search for your resume, and there was a database of job postings.

Despite its modest offerings, the potential was there! LinkedIn went public in 2011 and, over the next several years, continued to grow and develop. It adopted social networking features found on other platforms, such as a news feed, reacting and commenting on the activity of other users, and so on.

LinkedIn was rapidly becoming more than just a place to post your resume and search for jobs. It became a sophisticated *professional social networking hub*.

In 2016, Microsoft acquired LinkedIn for $26.2 billion, wedding their limitless resources and acumen with

LinkedIn's data and features. The site has continued to grow in size and capability since then, becoming something that every professional can use to land deal after deal after deal - if they play their cards right.

Section 1.2 - Growing With LinkedIn

To illustrate how important LinkedIn has become and how quickly it is growing, let's talk about legendary entrepreneur and digital marketing expert Gary Vaynerchuk. As recently as two years ago, Gary Vee, as he's affectionately known by his fans, didn't consider LinkedIn to be an important site for entrepreneurs to focus on.

In fact, in 2018, when Gary Vee released his "personal branding bible," *Crushing It!*, he outlined several major social media platforms that he considered relevant and explained how to use those platforms to grow a personal brand... and LinkedIn wasn't even mentioned!

LinkedIn wasn't even on Gary Vee's radar then, but he now advises that for business owners who want to grow their brand, LinkedIn is the TOP platform to use!

He wrote in a post titled, *5 Marketing Strategies for LinkedIn*, "LinkedIn marketing is something I really, really believe in for 2019. LinkedIn has transformed so much as a platform. Years ago, it used to just be for job seekers. People would post resumes and only connect with people they knew and no one else. Now, it's become more of a content platform."

He has noted that LinkedIn has a very high organic reach compared to Facebook, because it's a less mature, faster-growing platform and because it's focused on professionals and the business world. My own research agrees; LinkedIn has grown rapidly, and it's more relevant and powerful than ever.

But did you notice what part of the platform's history could be getting in the way of people using it correctly?

The keyword here is *resume*!

People still have the idea that LinkedIn is just a place to put your resume. This hasn't been true in years; the platform has completely evolved since those early days! Even so, LinkedIn's past lives on as a mistake that too many people make.

Remember our key principle above? You need to think about your audience when you use LinkedIn. Your profile, your about page, your photos, your tagline - everything is focused on attracting new potential clients.

It's not about YOU. It's about how YOU CAN HELP THEM.

This means that just throwing your resume up is not enough. You may have great credentials and a solid work history, but that doesn't matter if you aren't using it right. It's not about being impressive. It's about giving value to others.

The past is the past; we can't let it blind us to the present. LinkedIn is no longer a simple career website. It's a full-blown social media platform that can be used skillfully to attract a growing audience and establish your brand.

Section 1.3 - LinkedIn By the Numbers

In case you aren't completely convinced of what LinkedIn has to offer, here are a few more facts about the platform today.

- LinkedIn has more than 660 million users in nearly every country around the globe.
- The platform's app gets 42 million unique mobile visitors each day.
- LinkedIn is used in over 200 countries.
- It gains two new members every second.
- 25 million LinkedIn profiles are viewed every day.
- One in three professionals is active on LinkedIn.
- 61 million LinkedIn users are senior level influencers and 40 million are decision makers.
- 13% of LinkedIn users aren't on Facebook, and 59% of them don't use Twitter.
- There are 9 billion content impressions on LinkedIn per week, where only 3 million users are sharing.
- There are 1.5 million LinkedIn groups.
- 80% of B2B leads come from LinkedIn.

LinkedIn is a business-focused professional platform. People aren't looking to post cat videos or to be amused. When people log in to LinkedIn, they take on a business mindset and fully expect to make new connections, be pitched new ideas, find new talent, or search for employment opportunities.

When you market on LinkedIn, you're using this business-focused platform to connect with people, generate leads, improve brand awareness, grow business relationships, share content, and attract people to your website.

Think about how many new members LinkedIn has gained in the time it's taken you to read up to this part of the book - two per second, for every second you've been reading. LinkedIn has grown by hundreds of members! How many of those could be YOUR perfect client?

In the next section, we'll get down to the nitty gritty and talk about specific things that you can do to your LinkedIn profile to optimize it for branding and sales.

SECTION 2 - GETTING STARTED WITH YOUR PROFILE

"Communication to a relationship is like oxygen to life... without it, it dies." ~ Tony Gaskins

Your profile is the foundation of all of your activity on LinkedIn.

Every aspect of your profile, from the top to the bottom, should make people curious about you and eager to connect with you. It should showcase the value that you can personally or professionally offer.

This section is static, so you want to make sure that it's optimized, attractive, searchable, and ultimately helps the right people want to connect with you.

No matter what you're doing on LinkedIn, whether you're publishing articles, commenting on posts, or being seen in the "friends of friends" networking page, your profile's tagline will be visible. This is your digital first impression, and it can absolutely make the difference between people connecting with you or passing you by.

You'll find that this section is arranged starting from your background profile picture down to the experience and skills section. Implementing just a few ideas (especially the section about taglines) can greatly increase the number of connections you have and opportunities you receive.

Remember Our Key Principle!

As we look at each of the basic elements of your LinkedIn Profile, keep in mind the key principle we talked about earlier.

You want everything about your profile to attract potential clients and business partners. It's not about YOU. It's about what YOU CAN DO to help them!

Specifically, we're going to talk about

- Changing your profile visibility and your contact info
- Background photos and how you can choose the best background picture
- Your profile picture, including do's and don'ts on those all-important profile pictures
- The easiest profile picture tools that you can use to create the best snapshot
- How you can nail your tagline to make yourself irresistible to prospects

- Making the most hard-hitting unique selling proposition (USP) that answers the biggest question that all of your prospects have
- The secret to turning your about section into a curiosity driving client magnet
- What to say in the actual 'experience' section of your profile
- Leveraging your skills, endorsements, and recommendations to the best effect
- Adding that extra bit of flavor with interests

And finally, we wrap it up with some last-minute ideas to enhance your overall profile.

Let's get to it!

Section 2.1 - Profile Visibility And Contact Info

A good profile is made up of a lot of small things that add up to a big difference. It's like detailing a car. It's not a single thing that makes a detailed car beautiful, but when all those little things add up, the entire effect can be awe inspiring.

Before we start editing your profile, let's adjust your settings. Here's one I've caught more than once. Are you sure your profile is set to Public? If it's not, fix that right now! If people can't see you, they can't connect with you. Many people set their profile to private while they edit things and forget to change it back once they're done.

Here's another thing to check. Are you using a

memorable LinkedIn URL? The default URLs for LinkedIn profiles are generic and look something like this:

http://www.linkedin.com/in/michael-scott-245b5b42

By taking the time to personalize your URL, not only will it be easier for others to remember and share (think business cards), but it shows that you're paying attention.

Here's how to change these settings:

1. First, click on the ME icon at the top of your LinkedIn homepage.
2. Click "View Profile,"
3. Then click "Edit Public Profile & URL."

This is where you will edit your visibility. Make your profile public so anyone can see your profile, even those that don't know you. You can also edit your LinkedIn URL. If it's possible to do so, use your name. Something like:

http://www.linkedin.com/in/YOURNAME

If you have a common name, there's a good chance that this has already been claimed as a URL. If you run across this issue, try referencing your profession, a certification or specialization, or even your location to differentiate your URL from others.

Examples:

- www.linkedin.com/in/RealtorBobJones - In this example, since Bob Jones is a common name, the user prefaced it with his profession.

- www.linkedin.com/in/JohnSmithAPMP - In this example, John Smith includes a reference to his certification as a proposal and grant management professional.
- www.linkedin.com/in/DrSallyWilliamsGSU - In this example, not only was her name already in use as a URL, but someone had even taken the variant of putting a Dr in front of her name. So she differentiated hers by adding the university where she teaches at.
- www.linkedin.com/in/AAJohnsFreelanceWriter - You can also play around with using initials and different variations on your profession. In this example, Alice Johns used her first and middle initials and added her profession.
- www.linkedin.com/in/BigBallerShotcallerGreatestOfAllTime - **Don't do this.** Many people have funny or boastful Facebook URLs, but consider your audience. For every person who thinks this is funny or memorable, there will be several that won't even bother to engage with your profile any further. This should go without saying, but on a business-oriented platform, professionalism is key.

That wasn't so hard, right? You're off to a great start! Let's keep going.

Contact Info

At some point, every interaction that leads to a sale will be taken off LinkedIn and into the real world. Thus, you need to give them a way to contact you outside of the platform. This is what the Contact Info section is for.

Once again, from your LinkedIn homepage, click the ME icon at the top. Scroll down to the section for contact information and click "edit."

This section allows you to add:

- Your phone number.
- Your email.
- Up to three websites, such as your company site or professional blog.
- Your social media profiles and instant messenger information.

It's suggested that at the very least you have an email address and a website listed as contact methods.

Section 2.2 - Background Photos

What's the first thing people will see when they click on your profile? It's likely going to be one of the two photos that sit at the top of the page. There is a large background photo, sometimes called a cover photo, and then there is your profile picture.

Since the background picture is much larger, we're going to look at that first. Due to its size, it plays a key role in setting the tone for the rest of the profile. It can add personality and creativity to your profile, and it serves as an introduction to your personal brand.

Your LinkedIn profile is at the center of your personal

brand on the platform. Your images and the tagline will be visible all over the site, making that first impression for you, so make sure that when a potential client clicks through to learn more about you, they're seeing someone they want to engage with.

Let's look at how to pick a background photo and then how you add it to your profile.

Choosing A Background Photo

First, we need to make sure any photo we select meets LinkedIn's technical specifications. At the time of writing, these are:

- Format: JPG, PNG, GIF
- Dimensions: 1584 x 396 pixels
- File size: Under 8 MB

If LinkedIn's built-in editor isn't enough to fix your photos, I'll offer some suggestions in a few pages about tools you can use to improve them.

What kind of image should you use? Since branding is so personal, there are many varieties of appropriate images. It depends on what message you want to communicate to the reader.

Your background image could show:

- Social proof of your success (awards, recommendations)
- Your workspace
- A piece of equipment related to your profession

- Your local city or a local landmark
- An abstract or geometric piece of art
- Your workplace team

Each of these choices highlights a different dimension of your business. Which one is your ideal client, your favorite future customer, going to enjoy the most?

This may take some experimentation. You might need to A/B test your images over time to see how people respond to your profile. You'd be surprised at how subtle changes can alter the impression others get from a profile.

Stock Photo Or Not?

If you look around on LinkedIn at other profiles, you may start to see the same background images pop up on different profiles. A lot of people just search for generic stock images of professional-looking things and post them up. While this is an easy way to get started, I don't recommend it.

Why would you want to give the same impression as someone else? Your goal isn't to be average; it's standing out for the better. Stock photography may look great, but it's easy to copy. Even if you buy a photo through a service like Shutterstock, there's always the chance that someone else is using it. If you take your own photo, then you know it's yours.

If you have a smartphone (and these days most people do!), you'd be surprised at how good the camera can be for taking a background photo. Use the back-facing camera, as these cameras are almost always better than the ones you can use to take a selfie. Once you have a photo, simple image editing software can convert it to the right dimensions and size.

While you can use an image of yourself here, you're going to have another one just below it. If you're going to use a photo of yourself, make sure that it's one that clearly reinforces your brand, preferably an action shot. If you want to show that you're a business owner, be part of a group photo of your team. If you perform a service, show yourself doing that service or celebrating with a client about the result of that service.

If you go this route, don't stage it too much. Ask a coworker to take a candid professional photo of you. That will make your expressions and body language much more authentic.

Don't Be Too Generic Or Boring

Many people gravitate to "safe" background photos because they want to put on a veneer of professionalism - but that's not the way to brand yourself if you want to get attention. Remember, your profile page is your brand, and who seeks out a boring brand when they could be with one that stirs up positive emotions?

If you really can't think of anything, or if you want to have a placeholder image while you figure out the perfect photo, a piece of abstract geometric art is a pretty safe choice, as long as it is easy on the eyes. Make sure that you can legally use that image on your page; don't just snag the first image you find on Google Images.

Adding or Changing the Background Photo on Your Profile

How can you add a background image to your profile? It's pretty straightforward.

1. Find the ME icon at the top of your LinkedIn homepage and click on it.
2. Click on the option that says "View Profile."
3. On your introduction card, you'll find an "edit" icon. Click on that.
4. A pop-up window will say "Edit intro." In the top-right corner of your background photo, you'll see a little icon that will allow you to add or change the image.
5. Choose your preferred image on your computer. Select one to upload, and click "Open."
6. If you need to edit your photo for size, there will be an icon that appears to let you edit it to the right dimensions.
7. Click "Apply."
8. Click "Save."
9. Go to your profile and make sure it looks good to you. Try looking at it on mobile devices as well.

You've taken your first steps to make your profile much more attractive to your future clients. Let's keep going.

Section 2.3 - Your Profile Picture

Can you believe that there are some people on LinkedIn who don't have a profile picture at all? According to LinkedIn, just having a photo of yourself makes you 14 times more likely to get your profile looked at!

If just having a picture - any picture - can cause your profile views to increase, think of how many more you'll get if you make it a really good one! Let's look at what makes a good profile picture.

How to Pick Your Profile Picture

Sadly, while we may think that our achievements speak for themselves, we do judge people on appearance. You wouldn't show up to the office in the same clothing you'd wear to do yard work, because you know that people perceive you differently based on the way you look.

The way you present yourself in your profile image can help people get a positive impression about your professionalism before they read the rest of your profile. Also, your profile image will be attached to everything you do in LinkedIn, so it's worth taking the time to get it right.

Just like the background image, the same technical specifications apply, only the profile picture needs to be at least 400x400 pixels. This may seem large, but if you take a look around LinkedIn, you'll see a lot of photos that are too small, blurry, and pixilated. They don't make a good impression. Again, if you use the rear-facing camera, you'll get a better image.

Make Sure It Looks Like You

Now, what should be in the photo? The most important thing it should contain is YOU - looking like yourself! Unlike a Facebook photo, your profile picture is not the place to show off where you've been or to highlight you doing something cool. It's an ID photo.

Try to make yourself look like your standard business self as much as you can. Ideally, if you meet a contact in person or over video, you should look like you stepped out of your profile. If you normally wear your glasses, hair, or beard a certain way at work, your profile photo should reflect that. If you change up your look, change up your profile photo.

This also means that you should be wearing business-appropriate clothing in your shot. Putting on your work clothes will also help your face present a more professional appearance. It may sound weird, but it works!

What if you work from home and don't usually wear business clothing? In this case, you want to dress at the same level of the people you want to bring in as future clients. This will put you on their level and make them feel comfortable doing business with you. People are naturally drawn to people that have the same energy as them. If you want to appeal to a more elevated clientele, you may want to communicate that in your photos.

Keep your clothing simple. Patterned shirts and blouses will appear busy and distract the eyes from your face, especially given the small size of the profile picture. Make yourself the star, not your outfit.

Express Yourself Professionally

It's amazing to me how few people smile in their LinkedIn profiles. Instead, they look moody or angry or too serious, probably because they think it conveys professionalism. But you're trying to make connections here - you're networking!

A smile is welcoming. It shows new connections that you want to get to know them and that you're friendly. Make sure you put on your best smile in your profile picture, and you'll be miles ahead of all those sour faces.

While less common, it's possible to go too far in the other direction. You don't need to look zany or off-the wall to make your profile photo stand out. This also means no crazy selfie angles. Be friendly, but professional.

Frame Yourself Correctly And Look At The Camera

You don't want to be too close to the camera or too far away in your photo. It's an ID photo, remember, so you want a clear shot of your face. However, you don't want too much of your face filling up the frame either. A photo that's taken at too close a distance can look weird or even unnerving. A shoulder-up shot is a good distance, just like your work ID or your driver's license.

You also need to look at the camera. When we want to

identify someone, we look at their eyes. If you hide your eyes, you'll look like you want to hide - that's not what you want on LinkedIn!

Also, you're the star of the photo, so be alone in the shot! Group photos belong in the background photo section or somewhere else in your profile. Avoid using a photo where your face is cropped out of a larger group photo. You don't want to be surrounded by a bunch of phantom people. Likewise, you don't want the background of your photo to be too distracting.

Use Natural Lighting

If you think about it, a photo is just a collection of particular light patterns and intensity. Photographers obsess over light levels, and for good reason. Lighting can make all the difference between a great photo and a bad one.

If you take your picture inside an office with harsh fluorescent lights directly above you, don't be surprised when your complexion looks washed out and your face is cast in shadows. On the opposite end of the spectrum, standing outside in direct sunlight will have an equally unappealing effect.

What's the best lighting option? Try taking pictures near a window, so some natural light colors your skin in a soft, appealing way. Alternatively, take your picture outside on an overcast day, or near sunrise and sunset when the light is less harsh.

Finally, the position of the lighting is important. If the light is behind you, your face will be obscured and dim. Make sure the light is in front and a bit to the side of you, so your features are highlighted attractively.

When in doubt, take a lot of pictures in several locations and compare them later to see which has the best lighting. Don't be afraid to take tons of pictures; one of the greatest things about the digital age is that you never have to worry about running out of film! Take more pictures than you think necessary, then take your pick; there's bound to be a great one in there somewhere!

Adding or Changing the Profile Photo on Your Profile

If you have not added a profile image before, you'll follow the same basic steps for changing your profile picture as you did for your background picture.

1. Find the ME icon at the top of your LinkedIn homepage and click on it.
2. Click on the option that says "View Profile."
3. On your introduction card, you'll find an "Edit" icon. Click on that.
4. A pop-up window will say "Edit intro." And in the top-right corner of your profile photo section, you'll see a little icon that will allow you to edit the image.
5. Choose your preferred image on your computer. Select one to upload, and click "Open."
6. You'll be presented with a suite of photo editing tools. Use them to make your photo look just how

you want it to be.
7. You'll also want to set your image to be public in the lower right unless you have a very good reason to hide it from the public.
8. Once it looks good, click "Apply."
9. Click "Save."
10. Check your profile photo to see how it looks together with your background photo. Adjust either as needed until it looks the way you want.

Section 2.4 - Profile Picture Tools to Use

You may have a photo you really want to use, but it doesn't look as good as you want it to look. While this isn't a photo editing book, I can recommend some tools you can try to get the best out of your photos. None are expensive.

What are some things you might need to correct in your photo? They include light levels, color saturation, and things like red-eye that bring down the quality.

Be careful not to overdo it with filters; less is more, especially if you're working with photos already taken in good lighting. Remember, the important thing is that your photos bring about the proper impression you want your viewers to feel. As long as they do that, that's the important thing. There's even a tool you can use to find that out!

Editing Tools and Apps

GIMP is a free photo-editing software suite that has most of the functionality of Photoshop, although it has a steep learning curve. It's probably overkill for this task, but it's worth learning if you want to edit photos often as it's by far the most capable of the options I'll list here.

Windows computers often have fairly robust basic photo-editing capabilities. The Microsoft Photos app that comes with most modern versions of Windows can do everything from cropping to removing red-eye. There's also a variety of apps with different levels of capability in the Microsoft App Store. One highly rated one is Ultimate Photo Editor, an option that is free and provides a pretty extensive toolset.

Also, most smartphones have editing tools in their camera apps, and there are some great apps out there to use for photo editing as well. Here are some to try:

- Instagram has some great tools, and you can simply save photos from it instead of posting them to Instagram if you just want to use the app for editing.
- VSCO is free. It's great for adjusting lighting and comes with several free preset filters.
- Pixlr is free and works great for photo editing.
- Piclab is a free app with a great selection of filters and options for overlaying text. It's available for free and is very easy to use.
- Adobe Lightroom Mobile is a great option for people who have used Adobe products and

prefer them. It's got a robust set of tools for editing.

Find Out How You Look

If you've narrowed down your photos and can't decide which one to choose, or you need an opinion about your editing job, I have a tool for you. There is a service called Photofeeler that lets anonymous people comment on your photos for the feelings they convey. This is one of my secret weapons to choosing great photos for profiles.

When you upload a photo to Photofeeler, random people around the world will rate the image on how likable you are and how trustworthy you look. You may be surprised which photos attract the best attention! This tool can help you make sure your photo does the job it's supposed to do.

Once you have a good background photo and profile photo in place, it's time to move on to the text. You now have a good first impression. Now it's time to make your pitch, starting with your tagline.

Section 2.5 - Creating the Best First Impression With Taglines

When you run a search for people on LinkedIn, you'll see their profile photo, their name, and then a tagline. LinkedIn's default is to place your most recent job title as your tagline, but this leaves you at a disadvantage, as job titles usually don't say anything about who you are and what you actually do.

We're more than 'Co-founder' or 'Head Writer' or 'Accountant' right? A better way to do it is to think of it as your personal headline. That tagline is the first thing that people will see when they encounter you in a search. Along with the photos, it helps form that important first impression.

Also, your tagline is visible:

- When you like and comment on other people's content.
- When you post articles (we'll talk about articles in Section Three)
- When you post and comment in groups.
- When you come up in search results.

Wherever you go on LinkedIn, your name and tagline are right there. You want to make it generate enough curiosity in your audience that they want to know more about you and go to your full profile.

Your tagline should cover the following info:

- Who you are
- What you do
- The audience you're seeking to reach
- A strong selling proposition
- Your expertise and why you're a credible individual.

But here's the challenge. You have to do it in 120 characters or fewer! That's shorter than a tweet.

We're going to break down tagline creation into two parts:

- Keywords and optimizing your tagline for search.
- Your USP and how to express that succinctly.

Keywords: How to Love Search Engine Optimization

If you've ever used Google, you understand keywords: they're simply relevant words that people use to search for things. This is how all modern search engines work, and it's the same with LinkedIn.

- Recruiters and job seekers use keywords to find each other.
- Business coaches use them to find clients.
- Sales professionals use them to find leads.
- Entrepreneurs who want to expand their businesses use keywords to find... nearly everyone.

In other words, the keywords that you place within your profile make you more discoverable to your target audience, and this is especially true with your tagline.

So here's what you should consider regarding keywords.

First, they need to meet the expectations and needs of your clients. Carefully choose words that tell your clients what you have to offer them.

Second, consider which words your core audience would use to find you. The right keywords help make sure you come up as a relevant result.

Example: If you're a realtor, even if you own your agency, you probably want to include 'realtor' in your tagline even if that means leaving out 'CEO' or 'Agency Owner/Founder' because people looking for a realtor won't search for 'CEO.'

Put yourself in your ideal audience's head. What words are they searching for when they want to find someone who can solve the problems you can solve?

As an exercise, try a bit of competitive research:

1. Write down a list of keywords you would use to find someone like you. Try to come up with between ten and twenty.
2. Log onto LinkedIn and run searches on those words. See who comes up. Note which keywords have the most responses, and how their profiles look. Ask yourself:
    a. Would you stand out?
    b. Would you fit in with the group?
    c. Does that keyword make sense for you?
3. Look at the taglines of the users you find and see what other keywords they use.
4. Take a look at the job postings on the LinkedIn platform to see what kind of language they are using to search for people in your position.
5. Once you have a good batch of keywords, narrow down your list to a few top choices.

No matter how amazing you are, or how amazing your LinkedIn presence looks, it's meaningless if no one can find you through a search. You might have a funny or poignant thing in your tagline, but it may keep people from finding you. Figuring out your best keywords might take some time and work, but it will pay off.

By considering keywords for your tagline first, you're making best use of the valuable real estate in your tagline. Once you figure out your keywords, then you'll be ready to put that together with your USP.

Your Unique Selling Proposition (USP) Answering the Biggest Question Your Clients Have

Your unique selling proposition (USP) is designed to answer the biggest question that your clients have. This question is absolutely universal, ringing true across all verticals.

Ready?

What's in it for me? That's the biggest, most resounding question that you have to answer for your clients. This is where the rubber meets the road, and this is what your client wants to hear.

In the scant 120 characters that you have available, your USP needs to demonstrate 2 things:

- **Relevancy:** How does your product or service solve problems for your intended audience?
- **Differentiation:** What sets you apart from your competition?

Combined with keywords, your USP covers everything

critical in your tagline. To tie back to the key principle, this is where you first talk about how you can help your ideal audience achieve their aims through you.

For example: Let's say that you own a plumbing company, and you've received several industry certifications. You specialize in emergency residential repairs. Here, your USP practically writes itself.

- Certified Plumber Specializing in Residential Plumbing
- Certified Plumbing Expert with over a decade experience in clog clearing.
- Residential Plumber, certified in clearing the toughest clogs.

Your goal is to share your unique service proposition to appeal to your ideal audience: people with problems that you are best qualified to fix. What problems do your future clients need fixed? Why are you the best one to fix them?

Connecting the Dots

You've got your SEO and keywords, and you know the unique value that you offer your connections.

Crafting the perfect tagline happens when you combine the keywords with your unique selling proposition. You're ensuring people can find you and they know what you offer in one line of text.

Example 1: The Writer

Let's say you're an experienced freelance writer, with specialization in content marketing and web copy, and you love telling the stories of innovative brands.

Your proposition is: seasoned freelance copywriting professional.

Your selected keywords are: marketing, content, and storytelling.

Putting it together, you have...

Seasoned Freelance Copywriting Professional - Building Brands With Content Marketing and Storytelling.

If you want to drive it further home, you can say 'I build dynamic brands with content marketing and storytelling' or something similar.

Let's do another one.

Example 2: The Veteran Emergency Management Executive

Example two is a retired Coast Guard officer who is transitioning to a civilian career as an emergency management professional. Her experience in the Coast Guard was absolutely relevant to her value proposition. But how can she work that into her first impression when she's only got 120 characters to work with?

Her value proposition is: Experienced Emergency

Management Executive

Her keywords: hurricane relief, contingency planning, and Logistic Resiliency.

The tagline becomes: Proven Emergency Management Executive, Specialized in Hurricane Relief, Logistic Resiliency, and Contingency Planning.

But where does the Coast Guard experience come in? This is where the tagline, photo, and name can all work together since they all appear together. This individual can leave her tagline as-is and simply change her name and maybe her photo.

Let's say that her name is Kate Smith. If she changes her name to Capt. Kate Smith (USCG, Ret.) then she's displaying her military experience without using tagline real estate. In some cases, a retired veteran may be able to use a picture in uniform.

That's all there is to it, but you can also get creative to stand out from the crowd. Here are some tagline examples I like.

- Logistics Revenue Strategist - Working With Truck Companies To Maximize Revenue Since 2001.
- Operational IT Leadership - Specializing in transitions from strategy to execution - Herder of geeks
- Product Management Leader In Mobile B2B App Development - Co-Host Of 'The Week In B2B'

Podcast
- Creative Director And Digital Marketing Wunderkind - U.Kentucky Alumni Vice-President, Park Foundation Board
- Principal At AVX Media (And Yes We're Hiring) | Keynote Speaker @ Forbes Innovation Conference Tokyo 2019

You're always free to tweak your tagline, so don't obsess about making it perfect the first time. You can A/B test your taglines for a few weeks to see which changes get the most traction for you.

Note the use of the | character to separate out different sections of the tagline in many of the examples. This is a standard practice. You can also use a single dash if you prefer.

After people read your tagline and see your photo, they should have a general idea of what you do and what you can offer to them. What you've created so far makes up the first impression people will see on LinkedIn of you. Take your time with it!

Section 2.6 - How to Turn the About Section Into a Client Magnet

The headline is only the beginning.

Your about section, or your summary section, is where your profile will do the heavy lifting to impress your viewers.

If your tagline is the appetizer for who you are, your about section is the entrée.

This is the place where you're going to shine a million-megawatt spotlight onto what you've done, how you did it, and most importantly, how you can help others with those skills.

Here, you have 2,000 characters to draw your audience in a little deeper. SEO and the USP are **still** important. Your ideas still need to be stated clearly and simply. Save any long-winded explanations and details for when you've connected.

Don't just restate your tagline. You want to think about this area much like an opt-in page. In this case, you're not selling a specific package that you have. You're not selling your services.

You're selling yourself as a professional. The rest of it can come later, but the sole thing that you want to do here is get the person reading the message that you have in your about page to become curious about you enough to want to continue the conversation by requesting to connect with you or setting up a call on your calendar.

- What kind of transformation can a person expect to experience if they come in contact with you?
- Do you have experience at executing these transformations?
- What value can you offer that others can't?

Here is an excerpt from my current about section:

If you're an executive or entrepreneur and you're struggling to connect with your target market or generate revenue through social platforms and email campaigns, you're definitely not alone.

Here's where I can help.

I turn already great sales teams into content creators who generate massive revenue for their organization.

In other words, I help the good become great and the great get greater.

You can use content to -
- ✅ Develop likeable expert authority in your industry
- ✅ Engage your target market and let them discover your brand
- ✅ DRIVE HIGH QUALITY LEADS INTO YOUR SALES FUNNEL
- ✅ Nurture your already existing leads into a higher ROI
- ✅ Demonstrate your value to the marketplace, attracting new clients

Engage with the Ultimate Brand Messaging Consultant

You deserve to be renowned in your industry. You deserve to be the go-to authority with high-value prospects reaching out and begging to be your clients. To do that, you need to put yourself out there and make mouth-watering high quality content.

AND YOU MIGHT NOT KNOW HOW TO MAKE IT HAPPEN

That's okay. I understand first had how overwhelming and nerve-wracking content creation can be. After years of struggling, I'm proud to say that I figured it out

and have helped nearly a hundred organizations and individuals just like you generate unbelievably massive profits by growing their online presence and reach.
💰📈

You deserve to win and (As Gary Vee would say) CRUSH IT in your industry. You deserve to be seen as the expert. And I can help you make that happen.

So, what do you do right NOW?

📞 **SCHEDULE A CALL WITH ME TODAY** 📞 *so we can review your goals and objectives. Let's work together to transform you into a thought leader who uses email, video, and social platforms to create a consistently steady river of pre-qualified leads every single day.*

It's time to stop losing out on opportunities and turn the ship around by scheduling a call with me.

After this copy, I have all the ways that you can get in contact with me. This includes a Calendly link, which lets potential connections schedule appointments with me instantly. This app has been incredibly useful for me and makes scheduling a snap.

Your about section should *always* end with a call to action like the call schedule request I have above. Make it as easy as possible for them to contact you and move just a little further down into your sales funnel.

A word about the emojis in my profile. For many, emojis are written off as being too unprofessional to use in business copy. However, I have found that tasteful usage of emojis can set your profile apart... with a big emphasis on the word "tasteful." We've probably all seen a post online where people stuff in emojis left and right into a sales pitch, or just as a matter of course on a platform like Instagram. The goal isn't to turn our profile into a rebus!

In my example, I used them in three spots. First, as a way to draw attention to what I offer with the bullet points. Second, as a way to emphasize a key part of my message: my ability to bring power and money to other businesses. Third, as a way to highlight my call to action.

Think of them like hot pepper. You just need a sprinkle, and some people may not like it at all. Consider your audience here.

Finally, you also have the ability to add pictures and supporting information to demonstrate how effective your services can be and further move the needle with your connections.

For instance, you can add snapshots of the best testimonials that you've received and add them here. This is an effective way to reinforce what you're saying to your connections.

If your visitors are still interested in you after reading your about section, that means you've grabbed their attention. The rest of your profile will give them greater understanding about your history and experience - the stuff you expect on a resume.

You could say that the background photo, profile photo, tagline, and about section are the closest equivalent to a cover letter in a traditional job application. They're meant to grab attention and get the reader curious to learn more about you.

The next section, the professional and volunteer experience section, focuses on the resume part of your LinkedIn profile. This is the place where you can 'show off' and talk about what kinds of results that you've gotten for others, as well as the accolades that you've won.

Section 2.7 - Professional & Volunteer Experience

Your experience section, like the tagline and the about sections, should be tailored to attract members of your perfect audience. If they've scrolled this far, you've succeeded in getting their attention, and now it's time to give them proof of your accomplishments.

In recent years, there has been a shift in how employment history is discussed. There is now more emphasis on personal brand, rather than how long you've worked at a certain company. You're defined as much by your skill set and the projects you've worked on as you are by how long you've worked for a single employer or industry.

This is why it's important to talk about what you've accomplished for your employers (or your company, if you're an owner), rather than just job duties. By showcasing this, you show viewers of your profile what kind of results they might expect from you.

Like the tagline and the about section, you'll want to use the keywords you've gathered, as long as they fit in naturally. Don't try to stuff them in for the sake of having them.

An Example Of Experience

Let's say that you sell marketing packages to your clients. You're amazing at it, and you've been the #1 salesperson in the company for the past 3 years.

While that's an excellent accomplishment, that information doesn't really do anything for the prospect who's reading your resume. For all they know, you could have been the only salesperson on the team!

Instead, by reporting that you developed 15 sales funnels, each reaching over $2MM in monthly sales, you give your potential connection something they can visualize.

If someone could guarantee that they could bring you $2MM in monthly sales and your company wasn't doing that, you'd take the time to set up the call, wouldn't you?

These are the sort of things to highlight. Do this for each job that you choose to include, to the best of your memory.

If you find that there are old and irrelevant positions in

your work history, it's perfectly okay to leave those out of your experience section.

Volunteer Experience

While LinkedIn labels your job history as simply "experience," I'd prefer that they call it "Professional Experience," as volunteer experience is just as valid and helpful.

Volunteer experience often shows as much as professional experience about who a person is, if not more.

Volunteer experiences aligned with your personal brand are absolutely relevant to a good LinkedIn profile page. You never know when you'll share a philanthropic interest with a potential client, and oftentimes volunteer experience is just as demanding and educational as paid experience.

Also, when trying to break into a new field or a new market, it's not uncommon to use volunteer opportunities to hone skills, gain experience, and make connections.

Is volunteering for a soup kitchen necessarily an important part of your personal brand? Some would call it "filler content," but if it's a well-known operation or you wish to prove your dedication to philanthropy, it may be relevant.

However, if you're an attorney and you do pro bono work

on weekends with a low-income legal clinic, that's absolutely something to report. If you're in emergency management and you flew into a hurricane-ravaged Caribbean island two years ago to spend a month working on disaster relief, your potential connections should absolutely know that about you.

When you talk about volunteer experience, don't forget to include a description of the organization and your role. Don't forget to include non-profit boards! If you serve on a nonprofit board of directors or similar, that's a position you can leverage because it shows executive experience.

As when discussing your professional experience, focus on what you were able to accomplish rather than just your role and job duties.

Section 2.8 - Education, Certificates, and Courses

Education

This is one of the simplest parts of your profile. You can enter the highest level of education that you received, any courses you've taken, and any certificates you hold.

If the tagline, about, and experience section have done their work, you'll have people clamoring to get in contact with you. Here is the place where you can drive the point home with your education.

The education section might be an 'in' for people to reach out to you and connect with you. You might not have gone to school with the person, but going to the same school can give you a little boost when compared to other people of the same caliber.

Also, you'll find that in the 'networking' section of LinkedIn, you'll have the opportunity to connect with people who went to the same school as you.

Fraternities, sororities, and sports teams are also potential ties that should be included; people often like to do business with others that have similar hobbies or extracurricular activities. People are drawn to people that have something in common with them!

Licenses and Certifications

Many professions have licenses and certifications that can enhance your brand. If you have these, they should be listed. You can also add relevant online courses for vocational training.

If the certification is particularly prestigious, it's recommended that you highlight it in your tagline or your about section to draw attention to it. For instance, if you're in computer security and you have a CISSP certification, you'll want to highlight that.

Similarly, if your goal is to gain access to clients that require a security clearance, you don't want to bury that information at the bottom. Put it here and make it easy to notice.

Section 2.9 - Skills, Endorsements, and Recommendations

By now you're nearly done making your profile, but

there are just a few more sections to go. The next section is a crucial one.

The items in this section provide social proof from others about your competence. Here's how they work.

Skills and Endorsements

In this section, you can list up to fifty skills and ask people on LinkedIn to endorse your self-selected skills. To do this, navigate to your Endorsements section and click 'Add A New Skill'.

LinkedIn will automatically suggest skills based on your profile and the keywords you've added. There are also quizzes for common skills that can add special badges to your profile if you pass them, as proof of your expertise.

A great way to get endorsements is to endorse your connections for whatever skills you can. When you help others, they're more likely to return the favor.

Emphasize the skills that your audience desires and that you know you can get endorsements for. You probably won't need to add the maximum number of skills, as too many skills can look cluttered, and you don't want a bunch of non-endorsed skills. It's better to show off what you do really well than to claim to be "just okay" at a lot of things.

Recommendations

While skill endorsements are important,

recommendations are a more powerful form of social proof. They are a written statement by another person about your skills, much like a testimonial.

People can click on these and find out more about the person who wrote them, so when someone gives you one, they are using their reputation to promote you. Recommendations are prominently displayed on your profile, so it's good to get as many quality ones as you can.

Like endorsements, the best way to get a recommendation is to give recommendations. They will be strongly inclined to give you something in return. Another great time to ask for one is when you've done a good job for someone else; be sure to ask while the details of your great work are fresh in their mind!

Section 2.10 - Interests

The Interests section of your profile lists what LinkedIn groups and pages you follow. It's divided into three subcategories: "Companies," "Groups," and "Schools."

You can use this section to showcase two broad categories of interests, with advantages to each:

Personal Interests

Like Facebook and other social networking platforms, you can use the Interests section to list out things you enjoy and like to do.

How?

Let's say you love hiking. You can't just select 'hiking' and have it show up. However, if you join a group called 'Young Professionals Hiking Club' then that shows up on your interests.

Never forget the human aspect of business; it is more important than ever in our increasingly digital world. If I'm looking for a web designer, and I see two that I like, I may be more inclined to choose to work with the one that likes hiking because I like hiking.

Having a unique mixture of interests and hobbies may give you the edge in landing a potential job or client.

It's important to align this to our key principle; people want to talk about what interests them. Your interests should be an opportunity to connect with others and provide them that channel to discuss what you're both interested in.

Professional Interests

Within LinkedIn, you may see pages created by companies, schools, groups, and other kinds of organizations. If you choose to "follow" those groups, you'll be updated every time they post something new. This is just like following pages on Facebook.

The groups and organizations you follow show up in your Interests section as well, so people can see what you're following. You'll also automatically follow companies and schools you list in your experience and education sections.

Only follow people and things you honestly want to get updates from. It can be very tempting to follow companies and people just because you want to be seen associating with them, but if a new connection asks you about it and you can't reply, it will make you look bad. Again, don't lie!

Section 2.11 - Final Profile Tips

We've gone over how to optimize your LinkedIn profile using images, your headline, and your About section. We've touched on experience, your certifications, endorsements, recommendations, interests, and more.

Before we move on to the next aspect of leveraging LinkedIn—content—let's look at a few final tips that can help your profile stand out.

LinkedIn lets you add many types of content to your profile. Images, videos, and podcast episodes can add further credibility. Don't overwhelm visitors, though; less is more. Pick a few examples from your best work and use those to make your profile page pop.

Another thing to try is to reorder your profile sections so that the most important ones to your audience show up higher. When you're in edit mode, simply hover your mouse over the double-sided arrow in each section. Your mouse will turn into a four-arrow icon, at which point you can click, drag, and drop to another position on your profile.

A newer feature of LinkedIn is the opportunity to rewrite your profile in other languages, so that when someone who views LinkedIn in that language goes to your profile, your profile is in that language.

For those who speak more than one language, this is a great way to not only gain more visibility, but to show off your language skills. The option to do this is located just under where you changed your URL to the right.

At this point, if you've done everything I've suggested so far, you'll have a strong profile that you can start leveraging to get more clients than you ever have before on LinkedIn. Is there more that could be done? Sure, but at this point you'll need to experiment to see what works best for your industry and audience.

As you change over time and get more experience, you'll need to keep updating your profile to match your current level. Going over everything once a quarter is a good maintenance practice. You'll be able to find out about new features, update information, and respond to all the endorsements and recommendations you've received.

Next, we need to talk about how to leverage what you've just built. It's time to talk about content!

SECTION 3 - TURNING CONTENT INTO YOUR PERSONAL GOLD MINE

"You can have brilliant ideas, but if you can't get them across, your ideas won't get anywhere." ~ Lee Iacocca

Because of LinkedIn's history, a lot of users focus far too much on their profiles as the most important part of their presence. Yes, the profile is important - but leveraging that profile is what really gets results.

You've built your trap, and now it's time to bait it with content to draw people to your profile!

Did you know almost all the content on LinkedIn comes from just 3% of active LinkedIn users? If you can produce great content and meaningfully add to the conversation on others' content, you're joining an elite group.

There's an amazing amount of potential for those who create content for LinkedIn. So let's dive into how to do it right. You'll learn about:

- The two types of content posting in LinkedIn and when to use them.
- How to write LinkedIn articles so they gain traction and make you look good.
- How to post in a way that builds your audience instead of spamming them.
- Tools you can use to make your writing much more professional and accessible.

You'll also receive a handy checklist you can use for your articles to make sure everything is good before you publish.

Section 3.1 - Writing Content For LinkedIn

Articles set LinkedIn apart from other social networks. No other social network at the time of writing caters to long-form written content, with the possible exception of Medium. However, unlike Medium, you have a built-in audience with LinkedIn. Every time you release an article, each person in your personal network receives a notification.

If your audience engages with that article, then the people in THEIR network are told about it. A good article can spread like wildfire through LinkedIn and draw massive attention to your profile.

You can also create shorter pieces of content called posts. These are quite similar to Facebook posts. You can share things that interest you or jot down short thoughts you have that aren't suited for a longer article. I like to think of them as a way to keep your audience engaged with you between the times that you're creating articles.

On any content platform, it's only a small proportion of people who regularly create something new. Most activity is from people talking about and sharing the things people made. Just making the effort can attract attention.

I've met a lot of people out there who say that they can't write. That's fine. You don't have to write to create a post. You can post informative pictures, create videos, or other things. Posts are supposed to be quick messages that talk about what's on your mind at the time.

Here are a couple of guidelines for your LinkedIn posting:

Never write content just for the sake of content. This is a trap that many who are new to LinkedIn fall into. Always make sure that you have something informative, entertaining, or emotional to say to your readers. Put the value that you wish to give to them first.

Your content is your brand expressing itself to the LinkedIn audience, and maybe beyond. Make sure it's something worth reading.

The next section will explain some tips on how to accomplish just that. This is not a "how to write" guide, but it will talk about how to structure your articles and posts on LinkedIn for the best effect.

Section 3.2 - Crafting Thought Leadership Articles

To start writing an article, simply click where it says "write an article" near the top of your LinkedIn homepage. You'll be taken to the article publishing tool. If you've used applications like WordPress to create a post, this should feel familiar.

What Should You Write About?

Let's make this simple. **Write about what you know.** Articles can establish your authority in LinkedIn on a subject. They can help you draw a line in the sand about your opinions on a topic in your industry. Writing on what you know will help you better express your expert authority.

Avoid hopping on the bandwagon of what everyone else is writing about *unless* you've got something to add to the conversation and want to strike while the iron is hot. If you can quickly write a relevant article in time to capitalize on the latest buzz, you can get a big response.

If you feel like you don't have something to say, start reading the content that other people in your industry are making. Soak yourself in what they're talking about and think about it. Then talk about your own perspectives. Even if you just agree, you can talk about why you agree. You can talk about a situation in your business that proves your perspective. Case studies are always welcome, although you should be sure to respect whatever level of confidentiality your clients expect.

Article Structure And Length

You're probably already familiar with the structure of business articles from reading content online. On LinkedIn, the title of your piece is called the headline. This is followed by your article.

Articles are then broken up by headings, just like this book. This does two things. First, it makes it easier on the eyes. It is hard to read large blocks of text on a screen. Headings split up the flow of words and make them easier to digest.

Second, it lets people skimming your article get some idea of what you're saying before they dive in. The longer your piece, the more crucial headings become.

Let's talk about article length.

When Abraham Lincoln was asked how tall a man should be, he said, "Tall enough to reach his hat!" In much the same way, the ideal length of an article is **however many words you need to say what you need to say, with enough supporting material that your desired audience can understand your message.**

If your article is shorter than 1300 characters, it belongs in a post. Unless you really want to write like Seth Godin, famous for his pithy business articles, you do need some length. But not every article needs to be some 3000-word mini-ebook to get attention.

Headlines and Headings

Any copywriter will tell you that the headline is one of the most important parts of the article, as it is what will attract readers to your work. So, what makes a good headline?

Headlines need to do two things. They need to set up an expectation in the reader and a curiosity to learn more. The reason that all those stupid clickbait articles you see on Facebook work so well is because they do just that. They're crude about it, but they work.

You don't need to go that far (please don't go that far!), but the concept is the same. Here are some other tips that are specific to LinkedIn that will polish your headline ideas.

- Shoot for a headline that's 40-49 characters. These seem to do the best at delivering enough information to do the job without overstaying the welcome. That said, your article isn't necessarily going to bomb if it is longer or shorter.
- List-style headlines do work, even on LinkedIn! They're very good at arousing curiosity. Just make sure the list is something worth reading and avoid the clickbait-y second part (e.g. "You won't BELIEVE #8").
- Headlines that promise instruction or explanation do very well on LinkedIn. "How to" and "how" type headlines are always good.
- Avoid headlines in the form of a question. These

don't do well at all on LinkedIn.

Here's an example. Let's say you saw a service dog at work and have some thoughts about how it's related to executive authority. A good headline might read:

- "Twelve things CEOs can learn from service dogs."
- "What CEOs can learn from service dogs."
- "How to lead like a service dog: Advice for the C-suite."

A bad headline would be: "Do CEOs have anything to learn from service dogs?" If the reader already has an opinion, they'll skip right by it.

Finally, you may want to wait on writing your headline until after you've written your article. Quite often, once you've written an article, you may find it came out different from what you expected. Once you have the whole piece created, it's much easier to describe with a headline.

Headings tell the reader what the next part of the article will be about. They are guides for the eye to track and markers for changes in your topic. Good headings are concise and set expectations for what's coming up. Just like the one for this section. We're talking about headlines and headings.

The number of headings you need all depends on the length of your article and the flow of your ideas. Avoid putting in a heading just for the sake of putting in a heading. You can find articles that suggest a particular number of headings like five or nine, but forcing your article to fit a mold isn't the best way to get attention. Your ideas are what make an article spread, not because it looks great to a desktop publisher or a designer.

What about keywords and SEO? Yes, you can add keywords from your profile into your headlines and headings provided they make sense. However, your profile is going to be attached to your article. If you're taking the time to write something you know that's relevant to your audience, you'll probably have keywords built-in. So don't stress about it unless you really want to make sure your piece has a shot for showing up on a particular search query.

Images

Humans are visual creatures. We like images. It's why we spent so much time looking over background and profile photos. Your articles also deserve images. Like your profile, all articles can include a background photo that goes across the top, and you can embed photos into your article like any other piece of blogging software.

Images can powerfully inform and clarify your points. For instance, if you're writing a case study, you'll want to show some proof and an image is a good way to do that. They can also be there just to break up the flow of the text or to emphasize something. Any image you use should follow the same quality standards that we've discussed. They should be clear photos and have enough resolution to look good on different screen sizes. They should also be relevant to your piece and appropriate for business.

Always make sure you have permission to use photos! You do not want angry comments saying that you stole a photo in your history. *Copyright issues are no joke.*

Articles are also a good place for stock photography. If you do use an image with permission, give credit to the person in the caption or wherever you feel it's appropriate.

How many images do you need? It depends on the length of your article and the number of other things you're using to break up the text. At a minimum, I like to use a background image and one other image in my articles. Beyond that, go with what feels natural. Some experts say that you should have a certain number of images for a particular length, but that can feel artificial and forced.

Finally, a side note. Embedding videos is popular on other platforms but videos do not do well on LinkedIn *articles.* Save them for posts!

The Article Body - Reading Score And Tone

I don't know what you're going to write, nor do I know every audience and industry, but I can offer some general advice on making your article as accessible and approachable to as many people as possible.

The first is the reading level. Write as if you're writing for a 13-year-old. Yes, I'm serious! While you are writing for a professional audience, the more we have to think about hard words and sentence structure, the less we'll retain. It will also slow down our reading.

There was a study done in 2016 by Carnegie Mellon's Language Technologies Institute about the speaking level of American presidents. Most of them speak at a 6th-8th grade reading level, even presidents that we think of as particularly eloquent. Even Lincoln, at the high end of the spectrum, spoke and wrote at a 10th grade level on average.

Making your words and structure simpler doesn't mean your writing has to be "dumb" - and this certainly doesn't mean you should try to talk *like* a middle schooler. You can cover hard topics with simple words without compromising your professionalism.

How do you measure the reading level of your article? There is a standard test called the Flesch Reading Ease Test that you can run on your piece. If you have Microsoft Office, this is built into the spelling and grammar check, though you may have to turn on readability statistics. If not, there are tools online that can run the test for you. Readable.com is an example and has a lot of extra features, though it is a paid service.

You want to shoot for a score that's at least 65 or higher. The higher the number (up to 100), the simpler and more accessible your article will be. If you hit at least 65, you should be in good shape.

Another thing to look at is the tone of your article. This is the emotion that comes through your words on the page. Neutral language performs much better on LinkedIn than articles with a strong positive or negative tone. Try to match the tone of the Wall Street Journal or another business newspaper.

If you're not sure what I mean by tone, I'll demonstrate. Here's an example of neutral language.

Congress passed the Farm Subsidy Realignment Act yesterday, a new law that limits subsidies for corn farmers and caps total subsidies for these farmers at 90% of 2018's allowed subsidy claims. The law aims to reduce subsidy payments over time; by 2026, farmers will be limited to claiming no more than 50% of the 2018 subsidy each year. While the law was celebrated by fiscal conservatives as a smart move to cut the national deficit, farmers and the agricultural industry protested the decision, stating that the current subsidy levels are necessary to stay competitive with overseas agriculture.

Here's an example of a strongly positive article about the same post.

Congress finally passed some much-needed agricultural reforms this week, capping subsidies at 90% of last year's levels for this year and ramping down future subsidies over the next half-decade. By 2026, this law will cut our current subsidy payments in half. Corporate agribusiness has protested the new law as it will cut deeply into their profit margins, but the taxpayers shouldn't be giving handouts to agribusiness anyway.

Finally, we aren't paying for our food twice between buying food at the grocery store and giving our tax dollars to the farmers on the back end!

Here's an example of a strongly negative article about the same post.

Friends and fellow farmers, Congress sold us down the river. They have gutted our subsidy payments that were promised to us after NAFTA opened up our markets to cheap foreign produce that undercuts the prices we have to charge to feed our families. The President himself stated before the election that he was committed to maintaining a competitive American agriculture sector, and now he's broken that promise. As such, we're getting at least a 10% cut in subsidies immediately and they'll be cut in half within a few years. It's a dark day for American farmers, and you can be assured that we'll remember this when those jerks come up for reelection.

Now, this doesn't mean that it's never okay to write with emotion tempered with professionalism. However, on average, articles with neutral tones get more page views than positive or negative articles.

Not sure how to measure how well you're achieving the tone you're aiming for? There are web tools for that. Try the free Sentiment Analyzer tool that measures the tone on a scale from -100 (very negative) to +100 (very positive) using computational linguistics and text mining techniques. The pro version of Grammarly also has a tool for measuring tone.

If you're struggling to get your language into the right tone or the right reading level, don't stress out too much. Humans are not robots. Your article isn't going to bomb just because your reading score was 60 or you dared to express a negative opinion. Consider these tone and reading score tips as guidelines rather than rules that can make your writing more approachable and accessible.

Editing

Finally, once your article is written, you need to edit it. While you might believe that you have the most perfect article as soon as you've finished it, nearly every article you make will improve if you let it sit for a day and read it again before you publish it. This is a trick used all across the writing industry. If you are not a regular writer, you'll be amazed at what pops out.

Another thing to consider is getting someone else to read it. Professional writers do this too with their editors. It's easy to miss things or assume things that are clear to you but not to the reader. Even having a friend or coworker take a few minutes to look over your work can be a good idea.

If you're planning on publishing a lot of articles, hiring a professional editor to help you is definitely an option. Fortunately, you can find plenty of them on LinkedIn! Another thing you can do is use Grammarly to catch small typos. This is an online grammar checking service that is widely used. It's not perfect, but it may be helpful.

You'll also want to avoid the trap of over-polishing your articles. Some people get so caught up in the editing phase that they never actually publish. Once it's good enough, it's time to release it into the wild. This is another benefit of having someone look at your piece. They can help you decide when it's ready.

Publishing

Once you've written and edited your article, it's time to publish it. This step is simple; you just click the Publish button in the top right corner of the editing page.

Be sure that your edits are complete before you do this! Once you click Publish, your network will get immediately notified about your article. There is no preview. While you can go back and edit it afterward, there's always the chance that someone could see your first version.

Sometimes I'm asked when you should publish an article, and this is an important consideration. There is a lot of content out there. If you publish at the wrong times, your notification could scroll off of someone's feed before they get a chance to see it. It's not as bad as Facebook or Twitter, but it is possible.

Most people use LinkedIn during the workday, so the chances are high they'll see new notifications during that time. However, depending on who you're trying to reach, you may need to adjust for time zones or for unusual working hours. In the United States, 10 A.M.-11 A.M. is best because the entire nation is awake and within a time slot that usually has a bit of free time for workers, but again, it depends on your audience. Experiment.

Sharing

Now there's one final step, sharing your article. LinkedIn does some of this for you, but you can extend your article's reach. LinkedIn will prompt you to share what you wrote with your connections by asking for a blurb, a short introduction to the piece. It's similar to a metatag for a webpage if you're familiar with those, but you can also use hashtags to insert yourself into an existing conversation or try to start a new one.

Also, you can go to your article and click the share button next to your name. Clicking that will allow you to share the article to other social media outlets that you have in your profile. If you are friends with any influencers, you could mention them in your sharing messages and hope that they respond. By engaging them, there's a chance they'll send their audience your way.

You can write all the great content you want, but it doesn't matter If no one sees it. So don't forget to use these sharing features! Unseen content is useless for helping you reach your sales goals.

Tying content to your profile

Once you have several pieces of content, you can put up links to the best ones in your profile at the bottom of your About section. Links to your published articles will also show up in your profile in their own section, but you want to highlight the best ones. LinkedIn has built-in analytics for your articles, so you can see which have received the most views and comments to promote.

Section 3.3 - Article Checklist

Use this checklist to remind yourself of the things to think about when you make your articles.

- Choosing A Topic
    - Write what you know.
    - Engage with trending topics if you're an expert in the field or have a unique perspective.
- Headline
    - Strong, compelling.
    - Optimally between 40-49 characters long.
    - If possible or relevant, make it a how-to article or list-style article.
    - Do not use a 'question' headline.
- Writing The Article
    - Use appropriate keywords & phrases so the article comes up in search results.
    - Keep reading level as simple as possible.
- Tone
    - Neutral tones are best for most articles.
    - If you use a positive or negative tone, be aware of how you come across.
- Cover image
    - Relevant
    - Clear & appropriate
- In-article images

- Relevant
- Clear & appropriate
- Use captions where applicable
- Ensure all images are used with permission.
- Video/Multimedia
  - Don't put them in your articles. Use these for posts.
- Length & Layout
  - Length is appropriate for the subject matter.
  - Introduce white space
    - Paragraph breaks
    - Subheadings used
    - Images used
- Editing
  - Use Grammarly or other tools to edit and proofread.
  - Use a sentiment analysis tool to check tone.
  - When possible, have a friend or colleague read it and offer feedback.
  - When appropriate (non-trending or not time-sensitive) let it sit for a day.
- When to Post?
  - Tues-Thurs
  - 10 A.M.-11 A.M., or anytime during the workday of your audience
  - NOT on weekends or after work hours unless that is when people in your audience tend to be available.
- Publishing

- Make sure it's ready before you click publish! Double-check the checklist.
- Don't over-polish your articles.
* Sharing
  - Share on your LinkedIn page and relevant groups with an appropriate intro blurb.
  - Share on other relevant social media platforms.
  - Share on your personal blog, if you have one.

Section 3.4 - Using Posts

Articles are a critical component of becoming known as a thought leader. They are your main content source. But if you've ever written an article, you know they can take a long time to craft.

Posts, on the other hand, can be much shorter. There's a 1200 character limit. You can jot down a thought, record a short video, or share something from elsewhere on the internet just like many other social media platforms.

For example, Goldie Chan, founder of Warm Robots and one of the top content producers in LinkedIn, set herself a goal of posting a short video every day on LinkedIn for two years and gained enough of a following to be named a LinkedIn Top Voice. That's what gave her the courage to start her own agency.

Posts give you a way to engage with your audience

between articles or for sharing things that aren't as effective in full articles like videos. So what makes a good post on LinkedIn?

Just like articles, you need to figure out what resonates with your audience. Everything you post should have relevance. Facebook is the place to dump whatever you want. LinkedIn is much more selective.

Posts should be short, simple, and direct, no matter which medium you're using. If you need or want to go longer on some topic, save it for an article or create it elsewhere and then link to it through the post. Posts should be simple so that the LinkedIn audience can understand what you're writing about. Not everyone is an expert in your field, so explain jargon or include links that explain it.

How Often Should I Post?

Pick a posting frequency that you can be consistent with. If you're able to post a relevant, on-point post once a week, then post once a week. If you have a lot of thoughts and want to post daily, post daily. I wouldn't post more than that unless you have a lot to say about something very relevant to your audience. Too much posting will make you seem spammy. Leave your audience hungry for more!

But I Need Some Ideas On What To Post!

What kinds of posts do well?

Videos

Relevant videos are 5x more likely to start conversations in the comments section than other content.

Images and Quotes or Statistics

People love things they can quickly share to prove their knowledge, and images with statistics or quotes give off a sense of credibility. It's a low-effort way to drive engagement and stay in your audience's mind. Cite your sources though!

Product tips or best practices

Try putting out short posts highlighting little-known features in your products, or even celebrating new products. Even a short post helps build brand and product awareness.

Posts promoting other people

If you've got a team working with you, use posts to highlight members of your team. People on LinkedIn want to connect and build business relationships with other people, so help make that happen!

Documents

Do you have a document, slideshow, or spreadsheet that you've worked long and hard on? Now you can share that content directly with your LinkedIn audience! You can use this feature to build a portfolio of your achievements through posts.

Every audience is different, so again you'll need to experiment to see what kinds of posts people like from you. But as long as you try to put as much value as you can into your posts, you'll be heading in the right direction.

Section 3.5 - Excellent Third-Party Apps to Make Your Content Shine

Here is a roundup of the tools that we've mentioned so far for helping your content shine along with a few additional ones that I've also found useful.

Grammarly

Grammarly is a fantastic tool that quietly runs in the background of your web browser, highlighting grammar and spelling errors and suggesting fixes. It's not perfect, as it doesn't always catch subtle errors or when one uses the wrong word, but it eliminates at least 75-80% of errors. It also has a rudimentary semantic analysis capability.

Semantic Analyzer

This free tool will allow you to conduct a sentiment analysis on virtually any text written in English. The system computes a sentiment score that reflects the overall sentiment, tone, or emotional feeling of your input text. Sentiment scores range from -100 to +100, where -100 indicates a very negative or serious tone and +100 indicates a very positive or enthusiastic tone.

Headline Analyzer

Headline Analyzer by CoSchedule helps grab the reader immediately with headlines that are optimized for attention. This tool uses data from the web to analyze the optimal word balance and length for your headline to drive traffic, shares, and engagement. Brainstorm potential titles, enter them into the tool, and it will help you sharpen your hook and pull traffic from the net.

Pexels.com

Pexels.com is a free stock photo and video service. They have an extensive library that you can use to find photos quickly for your pieces. Be sure to look at the licensing agreements for whatever you choose. You may have to give attribution.

Shutterstock

If you don't want to worry about citations, you can buy images cheaply through Shutterstock directly from photographers. Your purchase will serve as proof that you have bought a license to use the photo for commercial purposes.

Google Alerts

Google Alerts is a great way to keep track of your field. You can set up alerts for important keywords so that when a news article comes up about them, you can respond as soon as possible, whether that's with an article or a post.

Keyword Optimization Tools - Storybase, Buzzsumo, SpyFu, and Answer The Public

The following four services are all fantastic for keyword research and can be a part of your process in developing and optimizing your articles. Each has its own advantages and price points.

Storybase can take a keyword and provide you with the most popular questions, words, and phrases associated with it, as well as detailed demographic data related to your keyword searches.

Buzzsumo can take that keyword and show you the most shared pieces of content related to it across multiple social platforms, either over the history of the platform or over recent periods of time. It also provides a 'trending score' that shows how quickly something is gaining popularity, allowing the user to see and anticipate content trends. I love this tool.

SpyFu is a fantastic tool for analyzing competitor strategy and success stories, giving you a detailed snapshot of their online presence and analytics that show what keywords generated the most SEO clicks, their Google AdWords history, and their inbound link and backlink traffic. It's a very useful way to leverage the experience and mistakes of other organizations to fine-tune your own strategy.

Answer the Public is a brainstorming tool that takes your keyword and generates graphical representations showing frequently asked questions and associated keywords related to that keyword. It's very useful for generating new angles to help rapidly iterate new content.

SECTION 4 - NETWORKING

"The way we communicate with others and with ourselves ultimately determines the quality of our lives."
~ Tony Robbins

Networking. That's the reason that LinkedIn was created.

The cofounder of LinkedIn, Reid Hoffman, was interested in creating a way "to help humanity evolve." In an interview with Business Insider, Hoffman says, "getting everybody better enabled through their network, to maximize your economic opportunity, is part of how you really advance society. And so that form of it really interested me. Now, some people approach it as professional networking."

LinkedIn makes professional networking easy. With over half a billion users, there are people from all walks of life from every part of the world. There are decision makers, college graduates, entrepreneurs, and company people on LinkedIn. And, with just a few clicks of the mouse, you can connect with them.

In the previous sections, we talked at length about building the foundation for people to connect with you. Your profile is designed to generate curiosity, to get people down from that 30k foot view and a little closer. When people look at your profile, they should know exactly who you are and what you can offer them.

Your profile, articles, and posts are passive ways to get people interested in you. In other words, you were waiting for the connections to come to you and ask to be connected. In this section about networking, we'll discuss how you can actively increase the size of your network.

We'll talk about:

- Connecting with your existing network
- Using your education to connect with people
- How to connect after someone has viewed your profile
- How to 'cold-connect' with potential clients
- Tips and tricks for highly effective intro messages
- Commenting and engaging with others on their posts
- How to engage in and have a presence in groups
- Continuing the conversation after the connect

Section 4.1 - Connecting with your existing network

"If you want to build a strong network that will help you move ahead in your career, it's vital to first take stock of the connections you already have." — Reid Hoffman, cofounder of LinkedIn, the Start-up of You.

Let's assume that you have no connections. Where do you begin? You've met a lot of people over your lifetime. From high school to college, your first job to your current job, your freelance work, and even in just 'daily life,' each of these people can help you form your starting network.

How to import the people you know

1. Click on 'My Network' (it's right next to Home)
2. On the left-hand side, under the 'Manage my network' box, there is a section labeled 'Add personal contacts'
3. By default, you will have the email that you signed into LinkedIn with. You can, of course, change this at your leisure.
4. Click on 'Continue'
5. A pop-up will come up, asking for you to give LinkedIn permission to trawl through everyone you've emailed to search for matches.
6. A few moments will pass, depending on the number of emails that you've sent out from that account, and you will be presented with a large listing of people who are in LinkedIn using the email that you've used for them.
7. Look over the list and choose the people you wish to connect with, but do not click the 'connect' button. Instead, make notes about who you wish to reconnect with.

If you've had your email for any length of time, you might enjoy the trip down memory lane. Projects long gone and outreach efforts of the past will most likely resurface with all of these individuals being placed into your 'contacts' list (within the 'manage my network' box)

As a note, if you look under 'contacts,' you will be given another opportunity to mass connect with people. A simple click in the upper-right hand corner of the box will give your friends, coworkers, and peers a very generic invitation to connect with you.

Don't send it!

There are two big reasons that you don't want to send out generic messages to your network.

1. Everybody knows a 'generic' request to connect on LinkedIn, and nobody wants to feel like they're part of an automated system.
2. If the relationship has lapsed a little, or you haven't been entirely close since you emailed them last, you'll want to provide some context of who you are as a gentle reminder.

The only time that it might be remotely acceptable to send out a generic request is when you know the person so well that it was an oversight that you didn't connect in the first place. Otherwise, just say no.

But, what should you do to connect with these contacts who you've done business with or talked with on a personal level?

If you've made a list of names, you can easily find your friends once more by searching by their name in the search box. The box is in the upper left-hand portion of the screen right near the blue in box.

The Degrees of Separation and Connection

From here, it depends on what degree of separation your friend is.

- 1st degree connections are already connected with you.
- 2nd degree connections are friends of friends.
- 3rd degree connections are friends of friends of friends.

And then there are those whom you don't know at all. With these people, you can send them an inMail which you can get with the purchase of LinkedIn Premium or Navigator. For right now, we're going to disregard these potential connections in favor of pursuing the free ones.

Remember that every new connection that you make puts you in touch with a potentially new set of 2nd and 3rd degree connections. If a group of people that you're connecting with is a tight-knit group, you might find that there are others out there who have already connected.

You can tell the level of connection that you already have with someone by looking at their name. It will say their name, then say 1st, 2nd, or 3rd. When you are networking, your goal is to transform them from a 2nd or 3rd-degree connection into a 1st degree connection.

How do you send a message?

1. **Click 'Connect'** - It's in blue right beside Message and More. If you're using the free version of LinkedIn, there's a high likelihood that 'Message' will have a lock beside it.
2. **Click 'Add a Note'** where it says 'You can customize this invitation' Here, you can give a bit more of the context and WHY you're connecting with this individual.

Here's a small note that you can send to people who have been added from your contact list. The people you've worked with will most likely already know the value that you bring to the table unless you've dramatically changed since the last time you talked.

Dear [connect first name],

Hi! Remember me? [Gently remind them of the project that you worked with the on / that you went to school with them / situation where you might know one another]. I think connecting with you here on LinkedIn would be a win-win, wouldn't you agree?

Thank you,

[your first name]

Once you're done, click send.

Depending on your level of familiarity with the person, the note that you send doesn't have to be incredibly formal. Just reaching out and saying 'hi' should be enough in most cases.

Section 4.2 - How to Use Your Education / Work Experience to Expand Your Network

In the last section, we talked about how you can start your network by bringing in the base of people with whom you've had email conversations. Since you receive both personal and professional email, chances are these connections come from all walks of life and provide a broad base of people to network with.

We're going to discuss a couple of ways that you can easily expand your network using your education and your work experience. Because you have this shared experience with these individuals, it should be an easier 'sell' to connect with you than if you were talking with them out of the blue.

The first way is through your 'My Network' tab.

The first people that you see in the main section of the 'My Network' tab are invitations which have come your way. These are from people who are interested in connecting with you. While only 3 show up at the top, you can click on 'show more' to see if there are more.

You can either ignore their requests or connect with them. Even if they're strangers, I'm more likely to accept their request if they send along a custom message that provides an inkling of how we could work together.

Underneath the connections, there are the people who also work at the same company as you. They are listed as 'People you may have worked closely with.' If you indeed work closely with them, you can get away with sending a generic connect message.

Below that, there are people you may know from the school that you claim. For example, I went to Auburn University, and it says 'People you may know from Auburn University.' There are only 8 people listed, but if you click the 'see all' tab to the right, there is a pop-up window which has a nearly unlimited number of people (depending on the school).

Going further down, there are many people with whom you can connect. These people come from every facet of your LinkedIn profile, including where you live, the groups that you're a part of, people who have a similar role as you, and more.

It's essentially an unlimited smorgasbord of people you can connect with. With each snapshot, you can see their tagline as well as the number of mutual connections that you have with them. Generally, the more mutual connections that you have with them, the more likely you are to know them personally.

Here's a sample note from someone who wanted to connect with me based on our experiences going to the same school. I think that it does nicely as an invitation (I did accept their connection request)

> Hi [first name],
>
> I'm a fellow [school or university] alum turned [job title]. I run a [business type], and offer [unique service proposition / tagline].
>
> I'd love to connect and share post-[school or university] experiences.
>
> Cheers,
>
> [your first name]

If you're specifically interested in connecting with people who are alumni of your school, have worked at your business, are in the same city as you, or some other criteria, you can conduct a search in the search bar and see who you'd like to connect with.

You'd use the same idea with the messaging, in that you would mention what you have in common with them and bring in the value that you can offer your potential connect. Remember that it's all about the value that you can offer them, rather than the benefit that they would bring you.

In the next section, we're going to talk about how you can connect with someone who has viewed your profile.

Section 4.3 - How to Connect After someone has viewed your profile

Everything that you've been doing up until now has been designed to attract visitors to your profile. If you've successfully transformed your tagline, summary, and experience into being more search engine friendly, combining that with your unique selling proposition, you should see some results fairly quickly.

Between 'Messaging' and 'Me,' you'll see the 'Notifications' tab which is shaped like a little bell. When you click on that, you'll get a report on how many searches that you've appeared in, who viewed your profile, replies to your comments, and more. This is a great place to see the results that you're after.

This information is also available on the left side of your screen, right underneath your picture and your tagline. You'll see two pieces of information: who viewed your profile and views of your recent post. By clicking on 'who viewed your profile' you will be taken to a window which shows your profile viewing stats.

If the people land somewhere within your already existing network and they haven't hidden it from view, you'll be able to see who has looked at your profile. If it has been hidden from view or they're not within your network at all, the platform will encourage you to purchase LinkedIn Premium to see who those people are.

You're still given a lot of information that you can follow up on, as 2nd and 3rd degree connections will be taking a look at your profile. And, the more 2nd and 3rd degree connections you have, the more opportunities you'll have to connect and make them 1st degrees.

Send these people a quick note to tell them that you've noticed, enforcing your value proposition to them. Here's one that was sent out for a content writer.

> Subject: Hi! You looked at my profile
>
> Hey! I noticed that you looked at my profile and figured that I'd reach out and say hi! It looks like we've got a few people in common, I'm amazed that we hadn't crossed paths before.
>
> I write blog posts for busy professionals, getting their voice out in the wild. So, I write things like [the post / article you just wrote] without you having to spend the hours researching and actually writing it.
>
> Always looking to talk with kindred spirits!
>
> [first name]

Of course, you want to write the request to connect in your own voice, tailoring it to your audience.

You have two things in your favor here.

1. They've just looked at your profile, so you're fresh on their mind. They now have cause to think about how you could benefit them.
2. You are considered friends of mutual friends, regardless of the relationship that you have with the mutual friend.

When you're working with 2nd and 3rd degree

connections, most of the interaction goes to reinforcing the fact that you two have something in common and stressing the similarities that the both of you have.

It's baked into LinkedIn's algorithms to put your similarities up front because it helps keep you using the platform and discovering the value of it.

The next section will be devoted to talking with total strangers using inMail. These messages have the possibility to be game changers, but they need to be approached very carefully as you only really get one shot.

Section 4.4 - Networking with inMail messages

InMail messages are messages which can be sent through LinkedIn to anyone who has an account on LinkedIn. These people do not have to be connected with you in some way, so you are simply doing cold outreach.

LinkedIn understands the value of being able to connect with anyone on the platform, so they have limited the use of inMail messages to those who have subscribed to LinkedIn Premium.

It's necessary to pick your battles when it comes to messaging people out of the blue, primarily because of the value that having these game changers on your side brings.

Before you send the message, study your target.

Read what they've recently posted. Learn more about what's on their mind right now. Remember that everyone wants something, but what we want can change in an instant. See if you can 'read' your prospect so that you can hone your inMail message to their needs right at the time.

Frame your 'reaching out' message in terms of the value that you can offer them. If you've been watching their activity, you've most likely got an idea of where their head is at, so you can use that in your favor.

Here's a quick and easy message that you can send to your potential connection, based on what they've been posting about.

> *Dear [prospect first name],*
>
> *I've been reading about your troubles with [situation that they talk about in their posts] lately. I've had that same problem, and I've had [really good specific success] with [unique selling proposition].*
>
> *I'd love to connect with you!*
>
> *Thank you,*
>
> *[first name]*

We've covered several of the ways that you can reach out to people and expand your network in the LinkedIn platform. In the next section, we'll be discussing some things that you can do to make your potential new friend want to connect with you.

Section 4.5 - How to Craft Highly Effective Intro Messages

LinkedIn boasts that 37% of all adults, or just over 1 out of every 3, use the platform to connect with people. This makes having over 500 connects a reasonable goal.

The introductory letter is an incredibly potent tool. This introductory letter forms your first impression and can make all the difference in the world whether people connect with you.

Drawing back just a little, it's sometimes easy to forget that the people on the other end of the keyboard are just like you: busy professionals who are trying to make deals and do business that expand their own interests.

Because of that, your connection message needs to accentuate the value that you bring to the table, and quickly.

Here are some tips that you can use to create highly effective introductory messages to send to your potential connections.

1. **Don't Be Generic** - Yes, this was touched on briefly before, but it really deserves mention again. Generic invitations to connect will nearly always be ignored / erased. They're incredibly

lazy and can be spotted a mile away.

2. **Humility and Thankfulness** - Even though you're the best thing since sliced bread, it doesn't need to be banged into their head here. The only thing that you're after with your letter is making the connection.

That thank you, regardless of how small a gesture it might seem, goes a long way. Thank them for taking the time to read your letter. Thank them for simply being there and being an inspiration.

Talk about the value that they offer to the world.

3. **Make It Relatable** - The moment that you provide context for your connection is the moment that you make yourself far more connectable.

Mention that you met them at a networking event a while ago and wanted to follow up on a speech that they gave.

Talk about how you went to the same school and ask them a question about the school that would demonstrate that you actually went there.

Say that you enjoyed the speech that they gave about a subject that you're interested in, following that up with a question and a request to connect.

4. **Be brief** - You have only a few moments to make a great impression, and while your tagline and your about section will do some heavy lifting, your respect for their time will also shine through.

5. **Be very specific** - Talk about the value that you're bringing them. Don't be afraid to give them parts of your own elevator pitch.

> Dear X,
>
> Hi. I read your last post about X, and it seemed like you were struggling with [struggle]. I've been helping business owners who struggle with [struggle] by using [this system] which tends to yield [benefit]
>
> Let's connect? I have 10am and 1pm on Wednesday available. Just click on [this link] to schedule your time.
>
> Thank you,
>
> [your name]

6. **Flattery gets you places** - It's true! Flattery will get you places, but it will also show your potential connect that you're not just a drive-by looking at profiles. Instead, you specifically want to have that person as part of your expanding network.

   To many, subtle flattery is refreshing because it shows that you took the time to look at your potential newest connect.

7. **Make it as easy as possible to talk** - If you're going to ask to take the conversation offline by asking for a few minutes to talk, be specific about

the times that you wish to talk. Set the calendar so that your potential connect doesn't have to think about their own schedule that much.

8. **Follow Up** - If you haven't heard from them in a few days, you have the opportunity to send another message to your possible connect. Remember that the people you're trying to contact are extremely busy and they might miss the messages and notifications which have been sent from LinkedIn. Take the time to craft another introduction letter and send it over.

9. **Don't Sell** - The only thing that you're selling when you're sending out an invitation to connect is yourself. All you want to do is grab their attention and bring them closer to you. You just want to connect. This isn't about the services that you offer; you're just starting a conversation.

Trying to sell somebody something immediately is like asking for marriage on the first date. All you're looking for is the micro-commitment of a tiny bit of time to press the 'connect' button.

In the next couple of sections, we'll be talking more about commenting and groups, two ways that you can use existing networks to your advantage.

Section 4.6 - Commenting Your Way to the Top

Engagement and communication is not a one-way street. The overall purpose for joining LinkedIn and connecting with people is to develop mutually beneficial relationships with them.

You want to create enough curiosity so that people want to talk with you, lowering them from the 30k foot view into your sales funnel.

In the LinkedIn dashboard, under notifications, you get a listing of the people who have liked your material, commented on your material, or otherwise interacted with that material. These could be either articles or posts.

By offering smart, thoughtful comments to the original poster, you are not only calling attention to yourself, but you're making yourself known throughout their network.

Smart comments are not the 'hey, nice post' types of comments, but ones which answer questions and otherwise continue the conversation that the original poster is having. One of the things I try to do when commenting on other people's posts and articles is to make that poster look even more amazing and smart than they already are.

One thing which you can do is use Gary Vee's $1.80 method for social interaction on LinkedIn.

Here's the idea in a nutshell:

1. Learn the top performing hashtags, and make a note of the top 9 of them.
2. Comment or otherwise interact with the top 10 of the posts which have these hashtags. In other

words, you're adding your 0.02 worth to the conversation.
3. Repeat.

What this does is bring your name to the forefront and make you associated with the top industry leaders in the field. As you continue doing this and continue talking, you will find that you're receiving more invitations to connect and more opportunities to expand your network.

Here are seven tactics that you can use right now to increase the value of your LinkedIn comments.

1. **Pick your posts and articles wisely.** The articles and posts which you comment on will show up in your profile under 'activity.' So, if you choose to comment on something, make sure that you don't mind sharing it with the world.
2. **Read the post that you're commenting on** - Sometimes, there are people who don't bother to take the time to read through the entire post to get the full idea of what the author is saying. Commenting from a place of ignorance is very noticeable and makes others want to stay away from you rather than network with you.
3. **Think about kindness, respect, and civility** - While what you're commenting on might be a hot-button issue, use your comment to be kind, respectful, professional, and civil to the original poster. At the end of the day, this isn't a war of words, it's a community of great people. Always remember the person on the other side of the screen.

4. **Be thorough and thoughtful** - When you're commenting on another post, think about the time and effort that it took to create the post in the first place. Only add something if you truly have something to add. Comments like 'nice post' or 'thank you for sharing' don't push the needle for you in any way.
5. **Ask intelligent follow-up questions** - Taking it one step further, ask the original poster and the commenters questions relating to the subject matter within the post. That keeps the thread going, inviting other people to comment on the post.
6. **Talk about others** - Want to keep the conversation going? Mention the other commenters or the author of the post or the article that you're commenting on. That's one way to capture the poster's attention and get on their 'radar.'
7. **Read your comments over again** - Before you hit the button to etch your comment into digital 'stone,' read it over once more. Read it out loud, if you like. Offering value is the name of the game, so you want to put yourself into the shoes of the person who's going to be reading this comment.

If you're having trouble finding posts to comment on, you don't necessarily have to use hashtags in your search. You can also search for individuals in your local area, people who went to your college, or simply people who are in your industry.

In the next section, we'll take a closer look at the groups that you can be a part of. We're going to be building on the information that was used here and taking it one step further.

Section 4.7 - How to Engage In and Have a Presence in Groups

LinkedIn shines as one of the premier business social networking platforms.

There's a group or a presence for nearly every industry and profession that you can think of, each with varying numbers of members.

Discovering your groups takes a few simple steps:

1. **In the search bar near the blue-boxed In in the upper-left hand corner of the screen, type in the keywords that you would use to find your target.**

   For instance, if you're a digital marketer and want to meet your peers, search for 'digital marketer' in the search bar and remember to select 'groups'

   Let's say that you've niched down and you're a digital marketer who markets for insurance agencies, look through groups to see if there are groups for people who want to market their business (there are).

2. **Look at the number of members that the**

group has. Ideally, the more people in the group, the better. The description of the group will give you a bit more insight about what the group is about. I usually try to stick with groups that have more than 1,000 members.

3. **Click on the name of the group you wish to join.** Read the 'About this group' section which thoroughly outlines what the group is about, and click on 'Request to join' if you feel that the group is a match for your needs.

Most groups that you'll be working with have an application process to join the group so that spammers are kept out of them. Nobody wants to get into a group and have people try to sell to them first thing.

Once you're accepted into the group, you'll be allowed to join in on the discussion as long as you follow the rules.

You'll be able to interact with the posts of others, answer questions, and provide immense value to your peers and potential new clients.

Not only that, but you'll have the opportunity to connect with members outside of the group, turning them into first degree connections.

On the right-hand side, you'll see a note which outlines the number of members in the group right near a button which says 'see all.' Click on that. You'll be presented with a list of the people who are in that group.

You can send messages to anyone who's in the group, even if they're not within your circle of connections. You have the opportunity to send 15 messages like this, so you want to make them count.

By messaging members of the groups you're a part of, you'll be able to expand your network, becoming great at LinkedIn.

What you'll find is that just making the connection isn't enough. You have to nurture that connection to the point where you're able to take your conversation out of the platform and into your sales funnel.

The next section will briefly talk about what you can do after making the connection.

Section 4.8 - Continuing the conversation after the connection

Up until now, we've talked about all the ways that you can make the connection with people, whether it's through gaining their trust in groups, creating mouth-watering articles, or having a customer-attracting magnet of a profile that explains your value to the world.

All of these activities are used to get that target audience to connect with you through LinkedIn.

The connection is only the beginning.

They're not buying customers yet. You've just gotten on their radar. They're at 30 thousand feet, and you need to bring them closer.

This section is devoted to how you bring them the rest of the way into setting the appointment with you.

And I believe in reciprocity... you've got to give, give, give, give, give some more. You've got to bring value to your audience.

I can't guarantee whether it will turn that prospect into a transaction, but I can tell you that I've had a LOT of luck using this method. What I do is about as simple as it comes.

In the first message, you flatter them by reaching out to them and say that you want to read more of their stuff. You mention that you want to connect with them. There are plenty of examples of 'intro to connect' messages spread throughout this book.

The second message, you mention that you want to break the ice. You talk about your unique selling proposition. Then you bring them a resource that can potentially help them with their work.

- "Here's an infographic that I use when I speak at conferences."
- "Here's a white paper that I use in this situation."
- "Here is a great checklist for moving your items."

Use your best stuff. And, if you don't have any best stuff, create it. It's well worth it for the emotional capital that you'll be investing in LinkedIn.

When they respond to you, respond back to them, "I'm so glad you enjoyed it. I hope that I can be of value to you in the future." That's it. No need to go further here. Just keep sending them value.

Send them even more value. Send them more resources. Ten, fifteen days later if you've sent them an infographic, reach out to them. "Hey, I hope that the checklist is working out for you. Here's another piece of information that we send out to our best customers."

It doesn't matter what you send to your customers, as long as it's valuable, intelligent, and related to your business.

Making the conversion into a conversation into a sale comes down to four steps:

- **Step 1** - Outreach
- **Step 2** - Bring Value
- **Step 3** - Say you're welcome.
- **Step 4** - Bring more value.

This type of thing has to be done consistently. Do this at least once a month, go to as many prospects as you want and bring them value. When they respond with gratitude, send them more value.

The second time that you bring them value, mention to them that you'd be happy to do a deep dive to help those prospects, to help them solve any problems which come up. Be in a giving mode and ask for the 10 to 15 minute call. Mention that you do this a lot and you want to help people remove those traps.

This isn't the time to be the cheesy sales person. This is the time to just do it the right way and give and give and give. By the end of it, and no, I don't guarantee this, but you'll find that you're making more and more wins.

The next section of this book is devoted to some paid parts of LinkedIn that you can use to accelerate your connections. By no means is it mandatory to USE LinkedIn Premium or Navigator. These tools simply make it more convenient to you.

SECTION 5 - ADDITIONAL LINKEDIN SERVICES

"Great communication begins with connection." ~ Oprah Winfrey

LinkedIn brings in some powerful and incredible services for the free user. In fact, you can achieve great things on the platform without ever investing a dime in analytics, advertisement, or information.

You can make deals, you can connect with others from around the world, you can meet your peers, discover your tribe, and more. It's been said that this is the "business version of Facebook," and you could practically stay on the platform all day, refreshing your feed.

If you're willing to make a relatively small monthly investment into the platform, you will be granted more access to the vast storehouse of data that LinkedIn has at its disposal. With certain paid options, you will be able to receive insights and be able to better connect with your prospects.

It's worth it to mention here that LinkedIn offers paid options for those who are looking for a new career or hiring new talent. As this book focuses on professionals growing their business, we're going to leave these two pieces (LinkedIn Career and LinkedIn Hiring) out of the discussion.

Instead, in this chapter we'll be focusing on LinkedIn Premium Business and the LinkedIn Navigator.

Let's get started!

Section 5.1 - LinkedIn Premium Business

According to LinkedIn, the LinkedIn Premium Business option allows you to find and contact the right people, promote and grow your business, and learn new skills to enhance your professional brand.

The yearly fee for this service breaks down to $47.99 a month. For those who plan to pay month to month, expect to pay $59.99 each month for these services.

For that investment, you'll receive:

15 InMail messages - InMail messages are very useful for those who are frequently contacting people outside of their network. The right connection message, combined with the stellar profile you've spent so much time fine-tuning, can put you in front of the right person who can help you make the deal of your dreams.

The InMail credits that you receive expire after 90 days, so it's best to use them as you have them available.

Business Insights - Here, you can receive deep dives on companies that interest you. You can dig into the people at a company, the types of people that they're hiring, and more. This will give you more insight into whether you want to pursue business opportunities.

Knowledge About Who's Viewed Your Profile - We talked in Section 4 (Networking) about sending a connect message to those who have viewed your profile.

In the free version of LinkedIn, you are only allowed to see the details of only some of people who have looked at your profile. Namely, the 2nd and 3rd degree connections. With those who are not in your network, only scant details will be provided.

LinkedIn Premium Business allows you to see all the people who have viewed your profile, regardless of their connection to you.

Browse Profiles - Profiles of people who are not in your network are kept behind lock and key. When you invest in the platform, you are allowed to look at others' profiles to your heart's content.

Online Video Courses - Successful sales people and entrepreneurs are always learning, reading, and taking courses. LinkedIn understands this, and offers "the most in-demand business, tech, and creative skills taught by industry experts" to LinkedIn Premium members.

Some courses offered:

- Content Marketing: Social Media
- Digital Marketing Trends
- Social Media Marketing: Optimization
- Success Habits
- Marketing to Millennials
- Programming Foundations: Data Structures
- Contracting for Consultants
- WordPress: Creating an Intranet Website
- Project Online Reporting with Power BI
- Excel: PivotTables in Depth

The next section will be devoted to LinkedIn Navigator, the part of LinkedIn that caters to the sales professional.

Section 5.2 - The Basics of LinkedIn Navigator

LinkedIn Sales Navigator is a powerful tool for sales professionals to harness the incredible data set hosted by LinkedIn and access the right people at the right companies.

Navigator provides you with an enviable toolset starting at $79.99 a month.

Sales professionals who use Navigator are:

- 51% more likely to meet sales quotas

- 80% more productive.

What does Navigator give you?

20 InMail Messages - InMail messages allow you to expand your network and impress people with whom you wouldn't normally talk. Since there are only 20 of them, they should be used tactically.

Sales Insights - You'll get to see who's been doing what at your prospect companies. You can see who's changed jobs, how your target company has grown, and more.

Advanced Search with Lead Builder - This is an incredible tool that helps you hone in on those deal makers and decision makers that interest you. You can also use the advanced search filters to find exactly the people you need.

Learn About Profile Views - You can see all the people who have viewed your profile, then send them a connection request through InMail. If they're in your network, you can send them a connection request or a message for free.

Unlimited People Browsing - Using their advanced algorithms, LinkedIn will show you profiles that may help you grow your business.

CRM integration - LinkedIn integrates with Salesforce and other CRM suites, saving leads and account info and logging activity within Sales Navigator. You can even append tags and notes to your information and it all syncs seamlessly.

'Deals' functionality - Deals allows sales teams to collaborate on their pipeline. It is a single place to access all details, including the people involved in the deal, allowing teams to collaborate on how to make the sale happen.

Deals includes a feature called "Buyer Circle" that visually represents and identifies all stakeholders in the client's decision process, including key members that may not have been previously identified. Sales teams can then develop strategies to influence key stakeholders and build relationships with the right people.

It also enhances the CRM integration, automatically entering information from Buyer Circle into your CRM package.

PointDrive Presentations

This functionality allows you to package and deliver sales content without requiring the recipient to download it. A key advantage is that LinkedIn reports who has viewed which parts of the presentation, enabling sales reps to more precisely target follow-ups.

TeamLink

TeamLink shows connections between prospects and any individuals at your company. This is a fantastic tool for relationship building; even if your sales rep can't land an appointment with someone, the guy in accounting who went to college with your prospect might be able to arrange the appointment for your sales rep.

While there are similarities between Premium Business and Sales Navigator, I'm going to refer to the LinkedIn FAQ to explain the difference:

LinkedIn Business is a paid subscription service that elevates the LinkedIn experience for an individual member. LinkedIn Sales Navigator, available for individuals or teams, is the best version of LinkedIn for sales professionals. Sales Navigator features a powerful set of search capabilities, improved visibility into extended networks, and personalized algorithms to help you reach the right decision maker.

I've used both the free version of LinkedIn and the Sales Navigator and have found quite a lot of value in both. You have the option to start a free trial and determine the value that any of the paid versions offer to you.

SECTION 6 - CONCLUSION

Thank you for taking the time to read this book.

We have put together a lot of great tips that'll get you on your way when it comes to presenting yourself well on LinkedIn.

If you think about LinkedIn as just one part of your sales funnel, you will win.

I personally utilize LinkedIn at the top and middle of my sales funnel.

The sales funnel can be thought of in three key phases: **exposure, likeability, and trust**. You can work your way down from the top of the funnel and go through these three phases.

Exposure

There are a lot of people in the world that don't know who you are. LinkedIn is a great place for you to get exposure to your ideal markets.

As you learned in this book, you can find your ideal markets by going into their groups and bringing value to them.

Your goal when it comes to LinkedIn is to create so much great content that it gets shared to create exposure for you as a salesperson and for your brand.

Likeability

You can create likeability using LinkedIn, whether you're creating your own organic videos, sharing great content, writing blogs, or making intelligent comments about information that brings value to your ideal customer.

The key here is to always be producing something which brings value to your ideal customer.

As you keep talking with your LinkedIn audience and keep creating, sharing, and producing content, likeability will gradually come into play. Your network becomes much more familiar with you and starts to know you very well.

Trust

When it comes to trust, that's going to be old fashioned. It's going to be a deep dive, a handshake, something that you can't do on LinkedIn - but you can pave the way for that trust with what you do at the top of the funnel.

People come up to me at conferences and events where

I'm speaking all the time and they're very, very familiar with me. They say, "Mike, I really liked that video." Or, "I really liked that share. I liked that information." They're more deeply involved and engaged with me than I am with them, because they've seen me, read my content, and perhaps even engaged with it.

Interacting with people makes it incredibly fun to be at conferences.

Recently I had a manufacturer reach out to me. I had never heard of this manufacturer, and yet they asked me to come speak at their national sales conference. If it were a ten-part process, they started at part 6 because they'd already been exposed to so much of my content.

They'd already gotten to the likeability phase. They already wanted to engage me. They were already a long way down the road and they called me up and said, "Hey, can you come speak at our conference?"

I never would have had that customer if it wasn't for consistently posting value on LinkedIn. Someone who liked a lot of my stuff happened to be connected with the manufacturer. He had no problems reaching out to me.

Can I promise that if you do everything in the book, this will happen for you? The honest answer is no. There's no way I can promise that to you.

But what I *can* tell you and promise you is that you will have more exposure to your ideal customer.

Can I guarantee that you will be more likeable? Not really. In reality, you're on your own for likeability.

But what I can say is that if you put out intentional, thoughtful, and intelligent content, people will appreciate it, and you'll build a lot of reciprocity with your audience.

You still have to be great at delivery, but if you are, this translates to sales.

If you look at it, you'll notice that the rules of the game haven't changed. Only the social platform has. You'll find that exposure and likeability will happen on business social platforms just like LinkedIn.

I hope that this book gave you some tips and ideas that you can use to help you through the top part of the sales process. I also hope that it brings you some great success.

Thank you again, and I hope that you have a kick ass LinkedIn day.

Here's how to get in contact with me.

- LinkedIn: http://www.linkedin.com/in/mikesweigart
- My Website: http://www.mikesweigart.com
- Email: mikesweigart@yahoo.com
- Mobile: 678-570-6154
- To Schedule a call with Mike Sweigart: http://www.calendly.com/mikesweigart

Made in the USA
Coppell, TX
18 September 2021